Vibrant Nation

What Boomer Women 50+ Know, Think, Do & Buy

What the experts say about *Vibrant Nation*.

"Let's look ahead ten or twenty years: The top marketing executives at the top companies and organizations are going to be the ones who figured out how to effectively connect with the hearts, minds, and wallets of Boomer women 50+. Here's the guidebook. *Vibrant Nation* combines powerful insights with practical advice anyone can use to increase success with this dynamic and critically important audience. Buy it, read it, and keep it handy. It's the key to your future success."

MATT THORNHILL, author of *The Boomer Consumer*, and Founder of The Boomer Project

"*Vibrant Nation* is a great read—very informative, very sassy, straightforward, doesn't miss a beat, perfect for all women, particularly those 50+! I loved it!"

AMY FERRIS, author of *Marrying George Clooney: Confessions from a Midlife Crisis*

"A crucial research book for marketing thinkers and doers, not data gatherers. Fueled by the voices of Vibrant Women over 50, Carol Orsborn and Stephen Reily assess and showcase a demographic often marginalized by mainstream advertising and marketing. If you want to know what is really on the minds of Baby Boomer women, don't ask them — just let them talk. That's what VibrantNation.com and this book let them do."

CHUCK NYREN, author of *Advertising to Baby Boomers*, and CEO of Nyren Associates

"Finally, someone understands that we're not seniors or Boomers or older women, but a vibrant nation of individuals passionately doing, laughing, and loving. We're influencers, consumers, and lifelong learners who feel strongly, live boldly, and love being in the company of other fabulous women."

KATHY KINNEY and CINDY RATZLAFF, authors of *Queen of Your Own Life: The Grown-Up Woman's Guide to Claiming Happiness and Getting the Life You Deserve*

"Carol Orsborn, Ph.D., and Stephen Reily have written an inspired and lucid manifesto for marketing success with one of the most powerful consumer groups today: women who are 'post minivan and pre-retirement.' The authors deftly dispatch lingering myths and build a case that this engaged consumer is in fact 'the Excalibur of demographics, tantalizing with the promises of untold riches and power.' But they go beyond mere myth busting. The authors provide creative and original marketing frameworks and insights with which leading-edge marketers can build powerful branding and advertising campaigns."

BRENT GREEN, author of *Generation Reinvention: How Boomers Today Are Changing Business, Marketing, Aging and the Future,* **and President, Brent Green & Associates, Inc.**

"If you want to sell to Boomer women, you have to know who these women truly are today. They do. Stephen Reily and Carol Orsborn get this better than anybody and supply innovative and profitable strategies for taking your brand to the next level with Boomers."

LEAH KOMAIKO, author of *Am I Old Yet? A True Story of Timeless Friendship,* **and** *Creative Strategist,* **LeahKomaiko.com**

"Women aged 50-70 are the real 'prime time.' They spend more than younger consumers and are eager to embrace new experiences and brands. They also are natural community-builders, and *Vibrant Nation* presents insights from one strong community these women have built together. This practical and inspiring guide is a must read for marketers who hope to connect with this Vibrant Woman's heart, mind and pocketbook."

MARTI BARLETTA, author of *Marketing to Women* **and** *PrimeTime Women*

Vibrant Nation

What Boomer Women 50+ Know, Think, Do & Buy

STEPHEN REILY AND CAROL ORSBORN, PH.D.

Book & Cover Design: JENNIFERDURRANTDESIGN.COM
Production & Prepress: JOSHUA PFEFFER | JOSHP.COM

Dedication

To the women of VibrantNation.com, pioneers changing
what it means both to be and to market to a new
generation of women 50+

Contents

Acknowledgments

This book, like almost everything at VibrantNation.com, is a team effort.

The on-site activity of our members has inspired the content, organization, and spirit of this book. Our members have inspired the book in other ways, too. Realizing early on that you only have to ask a woman to learn what she's thinking, we have included generous excerpts of dialogue, blogs, and content from the Vibrant Nation community to illustrate our findings. We are certain you will enjoy listening to the voice of the Vibrant Woman as much as we do!

Every great nation needs great leaders, and VibrantNation.com is blessed with the most passionate, organized, energetic team that ever helped govern a (sometimes unruly) body politic. We want to thank Marilyn Bryan, Cara Reynolds, Beth Blakely, Kate Chandler, Debbie Coleman, Frances Houston, and Caroline Heine for making this particular Nation a thriving website and a great place to work. Thanks, too, to Jennifer Durrant for a book design as lively and interesting as the women this book is about, and her invaluable assistant Joshua Pfeffer.

Carol Orsborn: On a personal note, my gratitude—as always—to my husband, Dan. This continues to be quite a wild and wonderful ride! Also, special thanks to my vibrant muses: Leah Komaiko and Beverly Olevin. And finally, I tip my (vibrant) hat to my coauthor and colleague, Stephen Reily. Not only I but every woman in this country who is or hopes to be 50+ owes you utmost respect and a huge debt of gratitude for your courage and vision.

Stephen Reily: People often ask me how a man in his 40s ended up starting a website for women over 50. The answer comes from two women in my own life–a grandmother, Gladys Reily, who continued making new friends and making the world a better place well into her 80s, and a mother, Molly Reily, who reinvented her own life after becoming a widow in her 50s and who at 80 now feeds the homeless in post-Katrina New Orleans, is featured by celebrity chefs in their cookbooks, remembers every grandchild's birthday, and goes out more than I do. They taught me that women can do anything at any age, and I hope that VibrantNation.com honors them. I am also grateful for the inspiration and support I have received from my colleague Carol Orsborn, both vibrant and wise. And finally, given the talent, affectionate spirit, beauty, and commitment to a better world that I see and enjoy in my wife, Emily Bingham, I can hardly wait to see the kind of Vibrant Woman she herself will become!

Authors' Note

Every woman who comments or posts content on VibrantNation.com chooses her own member name. In the context of this book, we have generally used the member names they chose but have taken the liberty of changing a number of full names to pseudonyms. We have also done light editing for typos and length in member posts.

Research for this book was comprised of both qualitative and quantitative studies over a three-year period. The foundational study "Well-Connected and Wired" was based on a lengthy online survey of 1,000 women 50+ with household incomes above $75,000 and college educations, selected from the general population. Subsequent survey results have averaged around 500 women 50-70 drawn from the 100,000 women who are VibrantNation.com members, e-newsletter subscribers, Facebook fans, and Twitter followers.

For complete reports of all research and studies undertaken by VibrantNation.com, visit the "VN Surveys" tab at VibrantNation.com.

Preface

BY MADDY AND KEN DYCHTWALD

For decades, we have been tracking two revolutionary trends shaping our world's demographic, economic, business, and social paradigms. The first is the aging of the population; the second is the enormous rise in the economic influence of women. Each in its own right generates monumental shifts for women and men alike and for the businesses that serve them. As this book illustrates, where the trends intersect—with women at mid-life and beyond—those shifts are seismic.

Women in their 50s, 60s, and beyond are breaking through the stereotypes of what it means to be an older woman. Where women could once expect to become increasingly marginalized from mainstream society as they aged, they are now gathering strength and influence. This female age wave is already stirring up far-reaching impact on the workplace, the marketplace, the family, and the world at large. We're getting to see firsthand what it looks like when the first generation of women who earned and managed their own money gets to rethink what work, retirement, and success can look like after 50.

It makes for a very Vibrant Nation indeed, 40 million strong in the United States alone. And a nation where women seem genuinely motivated to help raise the bar for other women of all ages, from all over the world. At an age when they might have expected to retire, many are instead engaged in reinventing themselves and the world around them. Rebooting their enthusiasm for a longer and more demanding work life, they are balancing the pressing need to fund their later years with a burst of postmenopausal energy and purpose.

This Vibrant Woman's role as breadwinner and influencer is only growing stronger. Out of choice and necessity, she continues to make and spend money, often purchasing goods and services not only for herself but for her partner, adult children, aging parents, and grandchildren. In many categories, she has become the number-one consumer of goods and services.

It is no wonder that one million of these Vibrant Women have found their way onto VibrantNation.com in the last year, seeking information and forming community under the radar of mainstream media. As a result, the conversations that take place on VibrantNation.com, a rich sampling of which are shared in this book, open a rare window into this new world, where both the trends of aging, women's influence, and experiential marketing converge in real time.

What we see are women who, as the authors aptly point out, are at once supremely confident—and sometimes surprisingly insecure. They work together to thrive in a lifestage for which they have few role models to show them how it's done successfully. They are the first generation of women facing the opportunities and challenges of how to age authentically long before they are old. Although no experts can answer the question of what the future will hold for these women, this book offers a three-dimensional view of what aging looks like today, not only for this group of pioneers but for the generations of women to follow.

Ironically, while demographers have seen the shifts coming since we first began writing about these trends in the 1980s, the media and marketers too often seem surprised to see them come true. While this book was written primarily for marketers, we suggest that anybody who wants to know about the dual, converging trends of the longevity revolution and the increasing power of women should read this book. What you will discover is a full-blown paradigm shift, one that neither marginalizes nor idealizes the experience of aging women, but rather, gives us what we all crave: information, insight, and above all an authentic peek at a world turned right-side-up. Enjoy your tour through the dynamic landscape of Vibrant Nation. Kudos to our colleagues Carol Orsborn and Stephen Reily. With their book as your guide, you're in good hands.

Maddy Dychtwald is Co-founder of Age Wave and author of *Influence: How Women's Soaring Economic Power will Transform Our World for the Better.* Ken Dychtwald is President and CEO of Age Wave and best-selling author of fifteen books on aging-related issues, including *A New Purpose: Redefining Money, Family, Work, Retirement and Success.*

Introduction

GREETINGS FROM VIBRANT NATION
BY STEPHEN REILY, CEO OF VIBRANTNATION.COM

This book is a guide for marketers who want to do more business in the Vibrant Nation of 40 million women in the years ahead.

VibrantNation.com is not the biggest website to gather women 50+. Facebook, with over twelve million members who identify themselves as women over 50, has that honor. But VibrantNation.com is the biggest website that gathers women 50+ exclusively. As a result, those of us who manage the site spend all day not just immersed in the world of women 50+, but listening to what they talk about when they know they are talking only with other women their age. We have our finger on the pulse of a fascinating, vibrant tribe of women who populate a Vibrant Nation almost forty million strong. This book is a guide for marketers who want to do more business in this Vibrant Nation in the years ahead.

THE ORIGIN OF VIBRANT NATION

When I went into a meeting five years ago to talk about eggnog, I never expected that it would lead me to launch the first and now leading website exclusively for women 50+.

It was just five years ago that I was sitting at a conference table with clients, when the light bulb first went off. In my role as founder and CEO of IMC Licensing, a marketing agency that develops new products for well-known brands, I was engaged in a conversation with a group of brand managers about whether a line of eggnog we had developed really fit the client's brand. Several young brand managers felt the product (already a best-seller) looked too "stodgy" for the 20-somethings they were trying to attract. The lead brand manager (not surprisingly, a woman in her 40s) then spoke up.

"While we spend 100 percent of our resources targeting people aged 21-29, I like that this product lets us speak to some of our most profitable and loyal consumers."

"Who are they?" I asked, curious. The team from IMC working on the project had never heard this fact.

She told me: "Women over 50."

Wow. Why would any consumer brand not only ignore but even fear any association with its most profitable and loyal consumers? And how long could a consumer brand succeed by doing so?

It didn't make any sense.

As I began thinking through the conversations I'd been having with marketers over the years, I realized that this was not an isolated incident. In fact, there was a persistent discrepancy between who was actually purchasing products and services and who was being marketed to. Over and over again, the numbers pointed toward the size and purchasing power of women at mid-life and beyond. In fact, I learned that women of the Boomer generation would represent (alongside Hispanics) the fastest-growing consumer demographic in the country over the next ten to twenty years. This was the same period of time in which the coveted demographic of 20-somethings would remain flat. And yet, there was so little interest in this generation of women that market researchers had not even bothered to study them. So I started my own research project.

A VIBRANT NATION REVEALED

Intrigued by the untapped potential, I organized three focus groups of women 50+ with above-average household incomes. Here is what those forty-five women taught me:

1. Women at the same or similar lifestage have a gift for connectedness. In two of the three groups, even before the moderator entered the room, one panel member revealed to fourteen other strangers that her marriage of 30+ years had recently ended. When I saw how these women were supported–again, by strangers with nothing other than their age and gender to connect them–I appreciated that this was energy just waiting to be tapped.

2. These women shared a positive attitude about the next twenty to thirty years of their lives. One word that came up repeatedly: Vibrant.

3. They also shared a negative feeling: feeling misunderstood by marketers and invisible in the marketplace.

4. This lack of recognition impacted not just their self-esteem but also their ability to engage in the marketplace as active consumers. One after another, they described needs that the marketplace did not seem interested in meeting.

5. Connectedness for these women meant more than friendship; it also provided the tools they could not rely on the marketplace to provide. At some point during these focus groups, every woman pulled out a pen to write down a recommendation or idea suggested by another woman. In fact, it was one of these women who actually mused out loud about how great it would be to have a community online—a place where they could all go 24/7 to continue the kind of dialogue that was taking place at that table.

Grun Roots

To make a long story short, we launched VibrantNation.com to the public in early 2009. These women wanted and deserved a nation of their own, a place online where they could tell their own stories, listen to the stories of other women like them, connect with each other, and breathe life into a website that was dedicated to responding to and serving their needs. For that reason, our real learning about Vibrant Women began after we launched the site.

VIBRANT WOMEN: A NEW LIFESTAGE

The most important lesson we have learned from our unique vantage point as the leading online community for women 50+: being a Vibrant Woman is entirely different from the lifestages that come before and after.

As you will discover by listening to these women's voices in the coming pages, somewhere around age 50 a woman begins seeing life in dramatically different terms than she did during the previous twenty years of adulthood, the years during which she was raising children, building a career, supporting a spouse or partner, and in many cases doing all three simultaneously.

As we watched women use and build VibrantNation.com we noticed that the topics they discussed most frequently were not just the topics that interested them most, but the topics that interested them most about their lifestage. Just like young mothers connecting to discuss strollers, colic, and potty-training, Vibrant Women connect to discuss such life-stage centered issues as going through menopause and the physical changes it introduces, finding purpose through work, calling upon spirituality and creativity to enhance their lives, and reviving (or ending) long-term marriages. With twenty or thirty years ahead, Vibrant Women are also focused on not only living their life to the fullest, but preparing for the best future possible.

WHY NOW?

This is not the first book to recommend that marketers pay more attention to Baby Boomer women. My coauthor, Carol Orsborn, cowrote one of the first books on the subject in 2006 (*Boom: Marketing to the Ultimate Power Consumer—The Baby Boomer Woman*). And shortly thereafter, Marti Barletta, a leader in marketing to women, wrote the inspiring PrimeTime Women, focused exclusively on women 50+. The world does not need another book explaining why it should pay attention to Boomer women.

But our understanding of these women has evolved over the last few years, in several ways. When Carol and Marti wrote their books, theirs were voices in the wilderness. After explaining to marketers why to invest in women at mid-life and beyond, the next appropriate step is explaining how to invest in her, factoring in all that we've learned about her, in all her depth, in all her complexity.

Complexity? Did I just say that women were complicated?

JUST BECAUSE IT'S A LIFESTAGE DOESN'T MEAN IT'S SIMPLE

I mentioned earlier that Vibrant Women expressed both confidence and insecurity about how they would make the most of the years ahead. The insecurity, I believe, comes mostly from the lack of recognition the marketplace and media have offered them. We have continued to see this expressed by our site's members, and marketers need to recognize it not just as a missed opportunity but for its implications regarding how they should engage these women.

Aging brings wisdom, but it also can bring new aches and pains. Gaining discretionary income for shopping empowers women, but being ignored by young sales associates can wear away at their self-confidence. Choosing to live by their own values can set women on a path to make meaningful new friends–if they only knew where to find them.

O ver and over, we see that the confidence of Vibrant Women can be tempered by uncertainties about exactly how and where to put their skills to work. That uncertainty makes a supportive community even more valuable, and it makes women even more likely to reward authentic recognition from marketers. We will have a lot more to say about this in the book, but be careful about messages that simplify this lifestage as either rickety and complaining senescence or total and self-assured fulfillment. Vibrant Women have a great sense of humor for many reasons, one of which is knowing that the healthiest response to their own combination of optimism, cynicism, wisdom, and insecurity can be a good belly laugh. Marketers who want to do business with this woman would do well to think about her less as a target and more as a friend—a friend who can be funny, inconsistent, both generous and needy, but always worth your loyalty, respect, and attention.

PART ONE

Inside the Nation:
A Map and a Compass for Marketers

1

THE VIBRANT WOMAN:

Who is she and why does she matter to marketers?

Ask a smart, upscale woman 50+ if she's a Vibrant Woman, and she will instinctively know what you're talking about. She doesn't need Webster's to tell her that means "pulsating with life, vigor and activity."

Ask a smart, upscale woman 50+ if she's a Vibrant Woman, and she will instinctively know what you're talking about. She doesn't need Webster's to tell her that means "pulsating with life, vigor, or activity." Or Cambridge Dictionary to describe her as "energetic, exciting and full of enthusiasm." She may tolerate a label like "mid-life," recognize herself as a Boomer, and even confess to AARP membership, but it is the word "vibrant" that most fully embraces the sense of who she aspires to be at this surprisingly dynamic time of her life.

This extended period of peri- and post-menopausal vitality is so new that neither social scientists nor marketers have provided a turnkey tag that has stuck. It's not simply "mid-life" or "middle-age"– stretched so far to the extremes of the mid-30s at one end and 70s at the other as to be rendered virtually meaningless. Nor is it "senior," "elderly," or "old." Neither marketers nor women themselves have embraced other proposals, like "primetime," "matures," or "crones." "Baby Boomer" and "Boomer Woman" have filled the gap, but they can do so only during this particular moment in generational history, when the age range of Boomer women (born 1946-1964) happens to coincide with this lifestage. But Generation X is already knocking at the gates of 50, even as the leading edge of Boomer women surge into the unmapped territory of the "new" 70 and beyond. Being a Vibrant Woman is a state of being that transcends any one fixed generation to represent a distinctive lifestage that is here to stay.

POST MINIVAN

Short of glibly announcing "you'll know a Vibrant Woman when you see one," we've taken a stab at a description that resonates intuitively with both the demographic and those who study her. We simply describe the lifestage as being women who are "post minivan and preretirement." As distinct from younger women, the Vibrant Woman has moved beyond the consuming tasks of raising young children, having finally emerged from largely defining herself in relation to the needs of others. She is no longer the

---

She is determined to use this time in her life to play an active role and make a difference in the world.

---

soccer mom toting the team around in her minivan, and, in fact, in a recent survey by VibrantNation.com, only 6 percent now own the ubiquitous vehicle so popular with women at a younger stage of life.[1] Preferring a sports car or sedan, the forward movement that the Vibrant Woman is experiencing in her choice of cars serves as an apt symbol for the greater degree of freedom and choice she now enjoys.

On the leading edge of the lifestage, the Vibrant Woman represents a departure from the women of previous generations, who traditionally experienced increasing marginalization with age. The Vibrant Woman is still working, out of both desire and need, concerned about making the most out of (and supporting) the longevity bonus of her elongated life span. She is determined to use this time in her life to play an active role and make a difference in the world. While she is clear-eyed about the new challenges that aging is bringing her way, she has a spirit of adventure and resourcefulness to both the issues and opportunities. And of utmost interest to marketers:

4

reaching new peaks as breadwinner, influencer, and chief decision-maker for her extended family, she has become the powerhouse consumer for the majority of products and services.

TARGETABLE MARKETING POTENTIAL

Of course, there are segments and nuances within the Vibrant Woman marketplace, which we will cover in depth in the coming pages. But this distinct period of extended vitality for women offers targetable marketing potential that deserves and demands distinct consideration apart from other marketing-to-women segments usually focused on younger moms.

Nor can it be captured simply by noting the scale and purchasing power of Boomers (who constitute the majority of the Vibrant Women demographic for the next 10+ years), data that researchers and marketers know well. Taking note of statistics has not generally translated into dependable marketing strategies or outcomes. Even marketers who do appreciate Vibrant Women as the Excalibur of demographics, tantalizing with the promise of untold riches and power, find her challenging to leverage. In many ways, she has proven to be more complex than other segments of the marketing-to-women world, as full of paradoxes as she is full of life.

Again, nobody disputes the purchasing power of this consumer. For marketers, the real question has not been how many of them are there, but rather, how do you reach and motivate them. In this regard, conventional wisdom has worked against making a special effort. On one hand, some marketers have mistakenly argued that when women hit mid-life, they lose their will to change brands, becoming deeply entrenched in old ways and behaviors that make them "not worth the effort." Equally misguided are those who believe that if you engage younger women, any older women who are willing to try new things will come along for the ride, either because they are desperate to recapture youth or because they will tolerate being taken for granted. Both assumptions ignore the evidence that we will be presenting throughout this book—that the Vibrant Woman has entered a dynamic lifestage of her own, deserving of specialized campaigns by marketers.

IS SHE TO BLAME?

There have admittedly been some spectacular failures: messages, products, graphics, and strategies that have made the effort to connect with her but have missed by a mile. Unfortunately, marketers who have made an attempt and come up short have tended to blame the unwieldy nature of the demographic rather than their own inability to crack the code. We will be presenting some of these cautionary tales to you in the pages to come. At the same time, however, there are an increasing number of savvy marketers who have come to realize that they can't necessarily apply what they've learned from observing either women from previous generations or women at younger lifestages. These are the visionaries, and we hope this book will inspire more marketers like them.

To truly connect with this Vibrant Woman, you have to listen to her. And not just to the words she's speaking, but digging deep beneath the surface to a bedrock of attitudes and beliefs formed by five or more decades of life experience. For example, while she is clearly defying the stereotypes of her mother's mid-life and beyond, neither is she always the confident revolutionary whom advocates describe. It is true that as a result of her elongated life cycle, her continuing involvement in the work force, and the impact of technology, she has largely avoided the flat-out marginalization from the mainstream traditionally met by women as they aged. She has transitioned into a dynamic period of growth, spurring her to "reinvent" herself at mid-life and beyond. But she does so in the face of several challenges, the first of which is having heard fifty years of negative messaging about what it means to be 50+. The second is an economy and financial system that make reinvention a requirement, and retirement something she may no longer ever expect to experience.

WRESTLING WITH CHALLENGES

Rather than the slow but peaceful decline into old age romanticized by previous generations, Vibrant Women are finding themselves wrestling with both the challenges and opportunities brought about by change. This is a woman who can be at once the center of her own universe and, moments later, surprisingly insecure. But whether this woman is having what she might refer to as her second, third, or fifteenth mid-life crisis, she embraces even the paradox of who she is with the same gusto she has brought to all of the lifestages through which she has passed, transforming each as she goes.

While neither as invisible nor marginalized as the older women who preceded her in mid-life, she nevertheless still smarts from the effort to get her fair share of attention and respect from the media, marketers, and society as a whole. Nobody's fool, she knows that marketers have found it easier, more productive, and probably more satisfying to target the "coveted" younger market. But then again, she amply rewards those who make the effort to successfully connect with her.

In fact, as the first decade of the new millennium came to an end, three phenomena related to Vibrant Women encouraged many marketers to give it a go. The first was the announcement, early in 2009, that women 55+ were the fastest growing of all the population segments on Facebook.[2] The second came out of the music industry, with the news that women at mid-life and beyond had lifted sales of Susan Boyle's debut album to become the most profitable album of the year. The third was the success experienced by VibrantNation.com, the leading on-line community for women 50+, which demonstrated that it was possible to do for this cohort what the marketing-to-mom sites do for women at a younger stage in their lives.

VibrantNation.com, which launched publicly in 2009, defied the prevailing notion that women at mid-life and beyond—despite the tantalizing numbers—were quite simply too hard to reach, let alone mobilize. In just one year, growing from its original base of 200 women to over 75,000 members, Vibrant Women suddenly had a unified voice, a forum they could trust, and the critical mass for them to know that whatever the subject matter, feeling, opinion, or need, they were not alone. What little "she" didn't know individually, "women like me" would supply via the growing bank of communal wisdom available to her 24/7 at the click of her mouse. Empowered, she began sharing her opinions on everything from the best moisturizer and latest fashions to investment strategies, dating, adult children, reliable cars, and the meaning of life. She was not only influencing her fellow members, but also the fifty to ninety-nine monthly contacts in her personal network.[3] Working the long tail of the marketing-to-woman niche, marketers suddenly had access to the thinking and influence of a word-of-mouth pool of over a million highly qualified, tightly targeted consumers with the clout and resources to make a real difference for products and services.

INFLUENCING THE INFLUENCERS

As a result, dismissive words such as "too dispersed," "too marginalized," "too set in their ways," and "invisible" have given way to clearerheaded conversations about how to influence the influencers. The seemingly impossible had been achieved: with virtually no media or advertising, this most promising of all the demographics had suddenly forged themselves into a coherent network of influencers.

If you didn't already know the impressive statistics, you probably would not be reading this book. But here are a few of the highlights about our 100,000 members that tantalize marketers:

> **The majority have household incomes of over $75,000**
> **Some 72 percent have bachelor and/or graduate degrees**
> **Each month over half have a personal connection with fifty to one hundred others**
> **Their connections are growing. They are getting more influential as they age.**[4]

And all this is duly noted before we even get into the statistics regarding the discretionary consumer dollars Boomer women wield. For instance:

> **They influence 80 percent of $2.1 trillion of Boomer purchases — more than any other segment**
> **A whopping 80 percent control their family's day-to-day finances.**[5]

As impressive as these statistics are, there is an even more compelling reason that marketers are standing in line to take their crack at Excalibur: the Recession. In an economy that sank virtually all other consumer segments, the Vibrant Woman has proven to be remarkably resilient. While she, too, has taken a hit, she has been less likely to be downsized than her male counterparts. With seasoned skills and deeper resources, she has brought a resilience to bear on challenging circumstances, proving to be the demographic most likely to start her own business,[6] go back to school for retraining, and open her home and pocketbook to her adult children, grandchildren, and aging parents. As the Recession has forced marketers to move beyond preferences and stereotypes to find and develop "new markets," Vibrant Women have suddenly found themselves in the consumer spotlight. In fact, this woman is proving for many industries to be "the last consumer standing." And with the breakthrough successes that are beginning to surface, it is increasingly clear that when the product and message are right, she will respond.

IMPLICATIONS FOR MARKETERS

Vibrant Women are more than ready to tell marketers what they think. In fact, at VibrantNation.com, our most popular newsletter featured the following subject line: "Finally, a skin-care company is listening."

The newsletter centered on a survey sponsored by StriVectin, the branded line of antiaging line products nicknamed "Botox in a Jar," asking Vibrant Women to tell them what kind of spokesperson they would respect. They were asked to choose between Tim Gunn (from Project Runway), Stacy London (from What Not to Wear), Carson Kressley (Queer Eye for the Straight Guy) and Sela Ward (best known for her role in the series Sisters). They chose Sela Ward, hands down, and that result told us that their most trustworthy skin-care spokesperson was another woman, and especially a woman over 50 who herself had beautiful skin and an engaging manner. Respondents were much less interested in hearing from a male spokesperson or an opinionated expert who hailed from another lifestage—no matter their level of notoriety or credentials. While the findings were interesting, the bonus take-away was equally valuable. We learned how willing the women were to engage in something, in this case a consumer survey, whose sole purpose was to provide them in the end with better marketing, products, and services. Impressed by the high response rate to the survey, we realized that unlike other consumer groups from "coveted" demographics who have become jaded by the attention marketers lavish on them, Vibrant Women are eager to help you get it right for them. And given how few companies are asking for their thoughts, listening to Vibrant Women doesn't just offer you a chance to produce more effective advertising. The effort itself makes for effective advertising. Vibrant Women will respond positively to a brand just for asking them for their opinion.

THE WHOLE TRUTH

Traditional research, like surveys and focus groups, are important tools for the marketer who wants to know how Vibrant Women think. But if you really want to dig deep to uncover their deepest aspirations, intimate issues, and real motivations, there's a caveat.

In a recent book, *Just Ask a Woman*, Mary Lou Quinlan, with colleagues from her agency, has explained why.[7] Her basic premise: For lots of reasons, women don't always tell "the whole truth" when they answer research questions. And until you can identify the difference between what a woman admits to—about her diet, her media consumption, her shopping habits—and what she actually does, much of the time and money you spend on research will be wasted.

Does this mean women, including Vibrant Women, don't tell the truth? Not really. Quinlan identifies a set of reasons why a woman can be both confessional and secretive simultaneously, mostly related to preserving the sense that she might actually meet all the expectations society places on her—and all the expectations

---

For lots of reasons, women don't always tell "the whole truth" when they answer research questions.

---

she places on herself. The brands that succeed with her recognize her goals but also sympathize (and sometimes even laugh) with her about the unlikelihood that she will ever meet them all.

Citing the example of a Boomer woman who might tell a researcher, "This is the best time of my life," Quinlan calls this one of her "half-truths." The whole truth, according to Quinlan, might sound more like "If this is the best time of my life, then why do I feel like my body is falling apart?" In the financial realm, Quinlan throws out one half-truth ("I manage my money well.") and then compares it to the whole-truth ("I don't want anyone to find out that I don't know my assets from my elbow."). Financial service firms who need the Vibrant Woman as their customer need to address the woman's self-consciousness about her own ignorance without making her feel dumb. The same is true in technology and consumer electronics, where insecurity about not knowing as much as they fear they should makes women hard for marketers to reach—but it makes it even more worth putting in the effort.

EMOTIONAL PARADOX

It's not that the Vibrant Woman wants you to address her fear of failing expectations ("the whole truth") alone; but if you think that her only feelings are positive/confident (about aging, healthcare, finances, or technology), you'll miss an opportunity to speak to her in a more honest, well-rounded manner. The fact is that Vibrant Women can feel both confident and insecure at the same time.

This is a level of complexity that surveys and focus groups may hint at but have a difficult time fully grasping or explaining. While Vibrant Women are happy to talk to marketers, if you want the complete picture, you will also want to eavesdrop on these women when they are talking only to one another. Of course, like women in younger lifestages, they are chatting about a lot of topics on a general social networking site like Facebook. But if you really want to dig beneath the surface to find out what's on her mind, you'll want to seek out the websites and blogs where she is connecting with "women like me." Just as new mothers head for sites like BabyCenter.com or Cafemom.com, Vibrant Women seek out sites and blogs where women 50+ talk exclusively to each other. Only when they feel safely surrounded by women in the same lifestage, in a context where they trust they will be understood rather than judged, will they bring up intimate topics, share their deepest aspirations, and provide glimpses into their real motivations.

Look deeply enough, and you will encounter the bedrock of

motivation upon which all successful marketing programs are built: the understanding that there is an overriding need among humans for recognition and respect. Even movie stars want to be recognized and respected for who they really are. But for a group like Vibrant Women, who get sparing recognition and respect in the marketplace, there is a particularly acute hunger to have this basic human need met. Meeting this need is both hard and easy.

MEETING A BASIC HUMAN NEED

It's hard, first of all, because it must be authentic. Vibrant Women can be cynical about marketers who say they want their business. They've heard the promise made often, but rarely fulfilled, so don't offer this recognition and respect lightly. You have to mean it, and you have to listen to them so that you can deliver it in a way that will be meaningful to them.

But it's also easy, because, when you really think about it, how hard is it to show a fellow human being– including women 50+–genuine recognition and respect? You have to mean it. And you have to do it more than once. The Vibrant Woman has been talked down to enough. While she won't be fooled, she will reward a company that earns her trust.

So understand first why the Vibrant Woman is a great customer and how she is different from who she was twenty years ago, and then tell her so. If she feels your authenticity, that you have really listened to her and that you genuinely care, she will reward you.

While she won't be fooled, she will reward a company that earns her trust.

So understand first why the Vibrant Woman is a great customer, and how she is different from who she was 20 years ago, and then tell her so. If she feels your authenticity, that you have really listened to her and that you genuinely care, she will reward you.

The Voices of Vibrant Nation

"As women in this Vibrant Nation, we know it's one of those right times to zestfully engage in exploring this next and best chapter in our lives."

ON AN INCONVENIENT AWAKENING
BLOG BY CAROL ORSBORN, "INSIDE THE NATION"

The popular term "reinvention" holds the promise of mastery over transition—but doesn't come close to describing the depth of experience many women 50+ are having these days. A better way to describe what many are going through would be "an inconvenient awakening"—something both to dread and celebrate.

This blog is for Vibrant Nation member *Wishin54*, and all of us who identify with her recent posting. *Wishin54* writes: "I am ready for a change in my lifestyle, job, location, etc. Any suggestions what to do?"

There they are. Six fateful words I have learned both to dread and celebrate: "I am ready for a change." For Wishin54, it's about life-style, job, and location. But virtually any one of us can fill in our own blanks. A better relationship with one's spouse or children, more financial security, better health...you name it. In fact, the possibilities are dizzying—but one thing is the same: Once you have uttered these six little words, there's often no turning back.

The popular term "reinvention," often used to describe such a period of transition—holds the promise of mastery over transition, but it doesn't come close to indicating the depth of experience many women 50+ are having these days. A better way to describe what many are going through would be more along the lines of "an inconvenient awakening"–something irreversible and profound over which one has apparently very little control.

Suddenly, what once offered security or comfort, or at the very least a sense that the world is orderly and makes sense, no longer suffices. The status quo begins to pinch and bunch up in uncomfortable places, as we wonder about the choices we've made in the past, the unfairness of fate, and the best way to navigate the rocky terrain-mostly in shadows–that lies between here and the better, but as yet unknown, destination.

For whatever reason-or apparently none at all-we become aware that what once used to work no longer does. Fate does not seem to care about our preferences regarding the matter. More than one of us has found ourselves wishing we could just put ourselves back to sleep, fluffing up familiar pillows and pulling our old reality up to our chins.

But even if we manage to hunker down deep into the feathers, insistent voices keep us from dozing off for more than a moment or two. And here comes another handful of equally important words: "Any suggestions what to do?"

I've only got one. Listen. Listen to the voice that stirs you up and refuses to let you nod off. There's no use reasoning with it anyway. And even if you manage to silence or drown it out for a moment with any of the many forms of denial, it will keep up until you pay heed. So you might as well do it now rather than later.

At first, the messages you may receive may be indistinct, vague, even disorienting. So do not rely on the voice alone. Seek the counsel of friends, read books, do research, meditate, take classes and workshops, seek coaching or professional help. But keep asking and keep listening until you know what's next for you to do.

While you may hope for easy answers and convenient destinations, content yourself with taking one baby step at a time and trusting that however long the journey, when you arrive, it will have been worth it. Even though it may not feel this way to you now, even yearning, fretting, wondering, and searching is forward movement, containing the seed of all that is to come.

Meanwhile, be open to sudden flashes of joy and clarity, breakthroughs, and convergences where apparently unrelated experiences seem spontaneously to fall together in sensible and meaningful patterns and where, paraphrasing Teresa of Avila, tears become comforting and tranquilizing, rather than disturbing or fatiguing.

Listen, and there will come a time when you will know what to do—and even while recognizing the inconvenience of your awakening, you will know that waking up is a good thing and something for which you can always give thanks.

ON THE PRICE OF REINVENTION
VN INTERVIEW WITH AUTHOR GINGER PAPE

Already very accomplished, The Vibrant Woman is pushing boundaries and struggling with the fear/anxiety associated with that.

When I started my own business, it was just like jumping off a cliff. I had a lot of fear to overcome, even though I'd had an excellent role model in my mother, a lawyer, and had taken plenty of risks in my own career up to that point. I had been a corporate officer of a major 100 company. I worked on Wall Street at a time when the bathroom for women was on a completely different floor than the one for men (I had to fight to get the bathroom moved to the same floor to be convenient for me.) I ran the Washington office of the American Stock Exchange. But when I wanted to start my own business, I still felt that fear. "How am I going to pay rent? How will I pay my employees?" A friend of mine eventually said to me, "Just do it. Just jump off the cliff." And finally, I did. Afterward I asked myself, "Why on earth didn't I do this before?" But the truth is, for me, it wasn't easy.

The tipping point, for me, were questions that we ended up including in our book: "At the end of every day, do you feel drained?

Do you think you need to be doing something more meaningful?" Before I started my own business, I was in such a spin-cycle mode. My child would ask me a question, and I would answer, but a few seconds later I couldn't remember what I'd said. I didn't know if I had even understood his question, because I was so exhausted.

Ultimately, jumping off the cliff was the right thing for me. But immediately after I jumped, I had a typical reaction: "Who am I if I don't have my job title and my money?"

Women can be better at repotting than men because they are used to wearing multiple hats and having to be flexible, both of which are very important. But on the other hand, many women have trouble overcoming the fear factor and their own lack of confidence. We need to give ourselves *permission* to repot

Ginger Pape, *Repotting: 10 Steps for Redesigning Your Life* (Hay House, 2007)

ON WHAT'S WRONG WITH ME?
FROM A CONVERSATION ON VN

Accomplished women 50+ are caught by surprise by the persistence of their insecurity. But they don't let their fear, confusion or frustration stop them—for long.

Fran Youn:
I've taught art for years and years and know that there's an artist within. But when it comes to actually putting brush to canvas, I'm nearly catatonic! I've got a book that's been rattling around my skull for over forty years, yet when I took a class thinking I'd get it at least started, all I could do was cry, cry, cry and had to drop the class.

What's wrong with me? I don't think I'm a person who takes criticism particularly poorly, and I can certainly bring out the latent artist in every friend and high school student I've met, yet I've put all kinds of obstacles in front of actually producing anything myself! I consider myself realistically self-confident and have a life I'm delighted with, yet this obstacle, whatever it is, stands in my way...

What the hell's wrong with me? Can anybody give me a good, quick kick of reality/perspective on how to tame this "beast" of insecurity (or whatever it is)?
ararebird:

I've been a self-taught artist for thirty years and have made my living solely with my art for almost all those years. Now with the economy, so many of my stores and galleries are no longer in business, and the ones that are are struggling. So, I've had to figure out how to market myself differently, and one of the things I've started to do is offer art workshops in my home. Women love to come here, and I create a very safe environment because I know how vulnerable we all feel when creating our own work. I have struggled with being "good enough" as a teacher. I have turned again to The Artist's Way by Julia Cameron. I've been doing the things she suggests to do (write morning pages and have a weekly "Artist Date" with yourself). It is helping me get past the fear I've had that I can't be an artist in this economy, where am I going with my work, is it good enough— the general terrors that seem to haunt "creative types." I am also not exaggerating when I use the word "terror," because it is terrifying to feel that you are not good enough, you can't have your dreams, etc. Perhaps because you teach others, you have an expectation for your own art that you feel you can never live up to, so it's terrifying to try. Perhaps there is a sadness in you that you haven't created your own art, and by taking the class, you got in touch with the sadness and you're allowing it to surface. Then, you place harsh judgment on your own reaction. If you were in my class, I would let you cry. I would tell you that you obviously need to do so. What is wrong with crying? Your inner being is expressing something valuable to you. I would love for you to be able to accept your tears, and the emotions that you are feeling, and let them be. No judgment–no criticism. I think if you were able to accept what you are feeling and experiencing, you would find that behind the tears will come the enjoyment of allowing yourself to be a creator. If that comes with tears, so be it. In answer to your question: Nothing's wrong with you. You don't need a quick kick–you deserve some self-acceptance and self-love. As I write to you, I say these things to myself, because making a living at your creativity is a challenging thing to do. I am working with being able to accept my fear and terror thoughts as just that—thoughts, and NOT the truth of who I am. I have also found great comfort from Pema Chodron. She is a Buddhist nun, and her speaking on her CDs has been like salve on my wounds. We all need, and deserve, love and support. I think it's wonderful that all these other women want to love and support you too. In our vulnerability is also our strength.

ON RESOURCEFULNESS
BLOG BY GAIL MARIA, "GONEPAUSAL"

***The Vibrant Woman faces her challenges with resourcefulness,
style—and more than a touch of humor.***

I had a fantasy about climbing Mt. Everest. I know I hate the cold,
detest the sight of snow, and have a fear of heights, but I could still
dream.

"Chirp, chiiiiirrrrp, CHIRRRRRPP!" Holy crap, what was going on?
I bolted up in bed and wildly looked around the room for a bird that
must be loose. I checked the clock; it was 3:02 a.m. My first instinct
was to burst into tears, and my second was to keep crying, but that
wouldn't stop the incessant chirping. Did I need a net or a gun?
Having neither, I summoned my trusty yellow lab to go hunting with
me. After all he's a bird dog and we had work to do. I wondered
if boxer shorts and a T-shirt were proper attire. Down the stairs
we schlepped trying to find the source of the shrill hideous noise.
I'm cursing, and the dog's half asleep and not on the scent. "Elliot,
where's the bird? Get him, boy! Go hunt."

He lay down and fell asleep in the living room while I stood there
trying to track the chirp. It was directly over my head, but it wasn't
flying. It was a round white object—the smoke detector. Crap. The
battery must have been low, but I was much lower, approx. 10 feet.
I stared up at it with venom in my eyes. I had to stop it or be driven
stark raving mad.

Chirp, chirp, chirp! "Shut up," I screamed for no reason other than
it made me feel proactive. There was no ladder, so I had to make do
with a chair. I scaled the chair in my bare feet and reached up...I was
2'8" away from peace and quiet. Now what? I needed more elevation
and fast. A fat phone book seemed like a solution. I set the book on
the chair and up I went. Curses, I wasn't even close. Two phone books
had to do the trick. Nope, I still couldn't reach the freaking thing.
Three phone books? I was getting dizzy, and my tower of books

was shaking, but I was closer. Chirp, right in my face as if to taunt my effort. Why wasn't I taller? And then an "ah-ha" moment struck me.

I ran upstairs and put on my cute Kate Spade raspberry red three-inch suede high heels. I knew I'd wear them someday! Fortunately, no one saw me in my climbing attire: striped boxer shorts, ratty white v-neck T-shirt, and heels. Look away or turn to stone! With trepidation yet determination I scaled the phone books. I had no climbing ropes mind you, or anything stable to hold onto. There I was solo-teetering on top of my man-made Mt. Everest. I could barely get my hand around the chirping monster and yank it off the ceiling. Victory was mine, and I did it without supplemental oxygen!

I put the detector on the counter and started to trundle back to my warm cozy bed. "Chirp....chiiirp, CHIRP!" I was going insane. How could this be happening? There it sat on the counter with no battery yet still chirping at me. I picked it up and held it in my hand, tears streaming down my face. "Chirp, chirp." Was I in Edgar Allen Poe's The Tell-Tale Heart? I was tired and broken. My only remaining solution was to get it out of the house. I dragged myself out to my car, threw it on the front seat, and slammed the door. Silence.

As I trudged back upstairs, I realized I had fulfilled my dream of climbing Mt. Everest. Remarkably I did it in my raspberry red Kate Spade high heels.

ON NO MORE APOLOGIES
VN INTERVIEW WITH AUTHOR SALLIE BINGHAM

Many Vibrant Women feel a sense of exhilaration at finally being able to pursue her own wishes/dreams/needs instead of "taking care of others."

Whether they are working full-time outside of the house or raising small children, the challenge for creative women is the same. We have no affordable child care and no federal subsidies for child care. It's a terrible burden on women who have great creative desire and ability but who have to make a living and/or raise small children....You need a space and enough piece of mind to be able to focus on your creative work for at least that limited number of hours. But it is grindingly difficult; there is no easy solution....

I'm still very involved in the lives of my children, but now that they are grown and all have lives of their own, my creative life is very different. I don't teach or work 9 to 5 any more, so I can devote all my time to writing. It's blissful. For me, my natural creative rhythm means that I write best in the morning. Finally, I'm free to go outside and hike, see friends, and do the philanthropic work that I still do.

Sallie Bingham, *Red Car* (Louisville, KY; Sarabande Books, 2008).

[1]Acxiom, "Member Research" (survey, VibrantNation.com, 2009), http://www.vibrantnation.com/stephen-reily-flash-forward/2010/02/18/post-minivan-pre-retirement-a-new-definition-for-the-vibrant-woman/.

[2]Justin Smith, "Fastest Growing Demographic on Facebook: Women over 55," InsideFacebook: Tracking Facebook and the Facebook Platform for Developers and Marketers, February 2, 2009, http://www.insidefacebook.com/2009/02/02/fastest-growing-demographic-on-facebook-women-over-55/.

[3]Carol Orsborn and Stephen Reily, "Well-Connected and Wired," VibrantNation.com, March 18, 2009, http://www.vibrantnation.com/assets/ 2680/White_Paper_-_Well-Connected_and_Wired.pdf.

[4]Ibid.

[5]While Vibrant Woman represents a lifestyle that transcends any one generation, at this moment of history, the women who are in this demographic largely coincide with Baby Boomers, the cohort born between 1946-1964.

[6]Ewing Marion, "The Coming Entrepreneurial Boom," (report, Kauffman Foundation, June 2009). Morebusiness.com.

[7]Mary Lou Quinlan, Jen Drexler, and Tracy Chapman, *What She's Not Telling You: Why Women Hide the Whole Truth and What Marketers Can Do about It* (New York: Just Ask a Woman, 2009).

2

WELL-CONNECTED AND WIRED:

Vibrant Women Online

Just as the mommy sites have proven that they can forge together a community of virtual strangers into a support group that fulfills everything from spare time to emotional needs, so have the Vibrant Women who have found each other online become a cohesive force.

I n less than a single generation, women at mid-life and beyond have transformed their 50s and 60s from a period of increasing isolation and withdrawal to one of connectedness and influence. Where their mothers and older sisters were removed from one another, too dispersed to be targeted productively by marketers, Vibrant Women have coalesced into a distinct and targetable demographic mass. In addition to influencing one another, they are the linchpin in the highly interconnected life of their extended families, friendship groups, and colleagues at work.

But how did this increasingly valued woman go from the margins of other groups to the center of her own in such a short time? The answer lies at the intersection of technology and women's liberation.

Before she achieved equality in the workplace, the woman at mid-life and beyond was subordinated at both work and home and could expect progressive marginalization as she aged. It was the rule rather than the exception that as her childbearing days came to an end, her circle of friends stagnated or declined and her opportunities to make new acquaintances shrunk quickly.

DRIVING THE WHEELS OF CHANGE

When women's liberation raised the glass ceiling at work, women began to ride– and drive–the wheels of change, with technology as their ally. With the postindustrial shift from brawn-based factory and field toward the technology-driven knowledge economy, women found that they could use brain power to close the gender gap, and they did so in unprecedented numbers.

Playing on an increasingly level field over the decades, she not only adapted to but mastered the workplace technology that made it possible. Her growing comfort with technology at work was

It didn't take long for this wired worker to realize that the same click of a mouse that allowed her access to resources on the job could also enlarge her personal horizons.

often less of a leap and more of an immersion, and one that suited women's innate gift for connectedness. It didn't take long for this wired worker to realize that the same click of a mouse that allowed her access to resources, knowledge, and people on the job could also enlarge her personal horizons. In less than a generation, she distinguished herself as part of the first generation of women 50+ in history whose already large relationship networks continue to grow as they age.

This unprecedented level of connectedness was one of the key findings to emerge from our first study of one thousand Vibrant Women.[1] Summarized in our report "Well-Connected and Wired," our research revealed that the average active thirty-day personal network for these Vibrant Women clocked in at a robust forty-six people. For the most highly connected third of these women, that thirty-day network included an average of ninety-nine personal contacts a month. Moreover, over half of the women in the study confirmed that their personal networks had grown substantially in the past five years.

A HISTORY OF CONNECTIVITY

In contrast to her mother and grandmother, the Vibrant Woman began laying the groundwork for this ever-expanding network early in life. Because she represents the most educated and mobile generation of women in history, the Vibrant Woman has had more opportunity and more motivation to connect with others than those who came before. Hers was not coincidentally the first generation to leave home in mass numbers for college, to backpack around the world, and later to follow her own and/ or her husband's careers to multiple cities. At every turn, she has shown herself to be active, curious, and both socially and externally oriented. Outside the bounds of her community of origin, she grew accustomed to adventure and new experiences, lifelong learning, and meeting new people. Technological advances, including the Internet, have allowed her to stay connected with others who hail from multiple contexts and geographies, everyone from childhood pals and college roommates, to former coworkers, boyfriends, and fellow travelers. Of course, she has also applied her networking skills to keep in touch with her adult children, as in turn they leave their own nests, and now with her grandchildren, who may be growing up a hundred or thousand miles away.

ADOPTION OF TECHNOLOGY

In contrast to the stereotyped image of the older woman balking at technology's door, the Vibrant Woman does not hesitate to incorporate electronic tools into her daily life. In fact, she is often among the earliest adopters of any resource or skill, technological or otherwise, that will either simplify and enrich her life or make it easier to connect with family and friends. That is why a wide range

She is often among the earliest adopters of any resource or skill, technological or otherwise.

of tech companies, from General Electric to AT&T, are investing billions into electronic-monitoring systems, orthopedic technology, and disease management devices. They know that if they can help a woman with a wide range of medical and care-giving issues (like keeping tabs on her parents) she will not only be the first to learn about and purchase it, but also to tell others. Other tech companies, like Skype and inventors of the Flip camera, have discovered an unexpected goldmine in the market of Vibrant Women, who embrace these products because they enrich connections with their children, grandchildren, and friends.

WHY IS ANYBODY SURPRISED?

As marketer and Boomer expert Brent Green points out, this woman has had to adapt repeatedly to changing technology over the course of her lifetime. Consider for a moment the list of technological breakthroughs she has already found the wits, courage, and resourcefulness to embrace over the years: handheld calculators, desktop computers, push-button and cordless phones, answering machines, VCRs, ATMs, cable TV, CD players, microwave ovens, photocopiers, faxes, DVD players, PDAs, e-mail, and Internet.[2] And the list keeps on growing.

FASTEST-GROWING SEGMENT ON FACEBOOK

By the time Facebook announced that women 55+ were the fastest-growing segment of all their consumer segments, the women of this Vibrant Nation had already provided us with both compelling evidence and illuminating statistics that something profound was going on. For instance, women in this segment were shown to be influencing the majority of the 66 percent of all computer purchases

---

She craves a wide range of tech toys, not just purchasing what she "needs."

---

credited to the Boomer generation overall. She craves a wide range of tech toys, not just purchasing what she "needs." Like many younger consumers, many either already own or would love to "treat themselves" to Blackberries, Kindles, and iPhones.[3] Unlike many of these younger consumers, when she purchases the electronics for her own use, she is probably paying for it herself. (When the younger consumer buys such products, he or she may well be asking a Vibrant Woman to pay for it.) In fact, in many cases, it is the Vibrant

---

It is the Vibrant Woman herself who is the "mom" whose approval is required before her adult children can close a tech purchase themselves.

Woman herself who is the "mom" whose approval is required before her adult children can close a tech purchase themselves.

It has become increasingly clear that these women have the motivation and money to adopt new technologies almost as quickly as younger demographics, and for many of the same reasons: they love products that make them feel more creative and connected to their friends and family. In our survey of Vibrant Women released in conjunction with the Consumer Electronics Show in 2009, respondents told us that 63 percent own an iPod or mp3 player; 44 percent own a GPS, and 30 percent use Skype and a webcam.

LIVING HER LIFE ONLINE

In addition to adding new products into her growing collection of electronic tools, toys, and gadgets, she's ratcheting up her on-line behavior, as well. Increasingly resourceful in her use of the Internet, she has shown that she has no issue visiting both topic-centered and mega-sites that are not demographic specific. For instance, in addition to her growing presence on Facebook, she is adding traffic to websites about everything from weather and the daily news to stock market updates and travel.[4] Her visits to sites such as Huffingtonpost.com, Classmates.com, WashingtonPost.com, and Weather.com are measured in the multimillions. And her impact on the statistics is even higher among those sites that are at least lifestage, if not gender, specific. These include the grandparenting sites such as Grandparents.com; websites like Caring.com that provide support and information around care giving; dating sites like eharmony.com; and the job-hunting sites for people seeking second or third career jobs, such as Encore.org.

Not just a passive observer, she is quickly adopting the Internet usage patterns of younger generations and posting content herself. In a 2008 study by AARP and the Center for the Digital Future, Boomer women and men indicated that half watch videos on-line, with 42 percent also posting their own videos.

As Vibrant Women grow increasingly comfortable on-line, we see them echoing usage patterns very similar to other demographic groups, specifically new mothers. The wildly popular world of mommy sites and mommy blogs like CafeMom.com and Dooce.com suggest how women use the Internet at any dramatically new lifestage. While

---

Not just a passive observer, she is quickly adopting the Internet usage patterns of younger generations and posting content herself.

---

new moms search terms like "breast feeding" or "cloth diapers," Vibrant Women are often finding their way to VibrantNation.com through a Google search on their own lifestage-appropriate concerns, such as menopause or empty nest. While their initial visit may be similarly mission-driven, looking for advice and guidance on a specific topic, once the Vibrant Woman witnesses the abundance of content opportunities as well as quality of interactions on the site, she is often inspired to stick around. At the most superficial levels, the Vibrant

Woman is beginning to drop in at such "vertical" websites in ways that recall her former browsing of the bookstore or magazine rack. For part entertainment, part fishing expedition, she is allowing both the

---

Women who have found each other on-line become a cohesive force.

---

value and pleasure of following her spontaneous whims and interests to lead her into unplanned interactions and purchases.

A FUNCTIONING COMMUNITY

Just as the mommy sites have proven that they can forge together a community of virtual strangers into a support group that fulfills everything from spare time to emotional needs, so have the Vibrant Women who have found each other on-line become a cohesive force. They are building trust in the sites, themselves, and each other, learning how much and where to participate and how to protect themselves. Along the way, they are discovering something they did not entirely suspect was possible—and certainly goes far beyond what the traditional magazine ever had to offer—community.

In fact, the very attributes that laid the groundwork for her proactive engagement with technology in the first place have fueled both her hunger and her willingness to experiment with the creation of communities on-line. For some, technology offers an immediate way to explore new professional opportunities and then to promote her own work. For an author, entrepreneur, or life coach, an on-line community offers a forum for thought leadership as well as growing a fan (and customer) base.

For others (and perhaps for most), an on-line community can offer benefits unavailable in her "off-line" world. Because of the Vibrant Woman's mobility, her devotion to professional accomplishment, or even her focus on raising children who have now moved away, "real community"–a community that gets her at her deepest levels, that makes her feel that she's not crazy or alone, that provides information and access to real resources, and that will support her various ventures and aspirations–has not proven easy for her to find off-line. Paying heed to her deep and eclectic needs–and not always willing to share her vulnerability with friends and family in the "real" world–she alternately seeks access to a larger, more comprehensive base of references and resources and the refuge of relative anonymity.

One of the biggest surprises in this dawn of the demographic-specific social networking sites is the discovery that there is not necessarily anything "virtual" about an on-line community. At VibrantNation.com, you will find women talking about real, useful, fun, and vulnerable subjects at all hours of the day and night. As one member wrote: "To know that I am not alone in this indescribable unsettled feeling is a great relief to me today."

Vibrant Women on-line help each other on difficult-to-write résumés, point each other toward the drugstore version of the $350 moisturizer that works just as well, and check up on the results of one another's recent medical tests. They're buying each others' books, traveling together, and figuring out how to pool resources on a wide range of subjects, from where to invest to whether they should buy property together. At a stage in their life when previous generations became increasingly marginalized and powerless, Vibrant Women are reaping the ultimate rewards of a lifelong engagement with technology. They are finding not only their own voices but each other on-line.

IMPLICATIONS FOR MARKETERS

We still occasionally hear from marketers who ask, "Are Boomer women really on-line?" We're not sure whether such smart people actually doubt the studies that show how many hours Boomers are spending on-line or whether they suspect that women 50+ are looking in at the web occasionally but still relying on other conversational formats (like book groups), other media (like magazines), and other distribution channels (like bricks-and-mortar) as the primary venue for influencing the decision on what and where to buy. Maybe they resist believing these facts because it was so much easier to reach Boomer women when marketers could find them in the old familiar spots like newspapers and network television.

REVISITING THE AGE DIVIDE

If you share any of these doubts and suspicions, it's time to let them go. Women, and especially Vibrant Women, are researching, reading, connecting, shopping, and interacting in surprisingly nonstereotypical ways on-line. Such use just hasn't gotten much attention, but those who are enjoying success with this demographic know they've tapped a veritable gold mine…often with virtually no

> If you are looking for the better-educated Vibrant Women with more discretionary income, you will find her on-line.

competition. AARP.com's gaming site, for example, has been one of its most popular features (if not its most popular) for years. And women are spending hours at a time on Facebook not just to connect with friends but to engage in virtual games like Farmville as well.

Rather than an "age divide" in Internet use (the assumption that youth equates with Internet usage), every study we have seen confirms that the greater divide is over socioeconomic status. Internet usage is more associated with household income and educational levels than with age. If you are looking for the better-educated Vibrant Women with more discretionary income, you will find her on-line.

The Pew Internet & American Life Project has helped us better understand the rapid and dramatic changes in this space. Over the last two years, Boomers have come to use the Internet in the varied ways that younger consumers did in the early 2000s. Over the same period, they came to use social media like younger consumers, too. As of the turn of the first decade of the new millennium, half of all Boomers regularly maintain social networking site profiles and 75 percent of Boomers visit social media sites at least one time per week.

HOW TO ENGAGE HER ONLINE

As with other demographics, on-line advertising works better for Vibrant Women when you also have something to sell her on-line. Here are a few basic guidelines to motivate her interest and purchase:

1. Use the right imagery. While the Vibrant Woman doesn't expect to see ads that feature only women 50+, she does expect to see you acknowledge that women 50+ matter. Citi's Women & Co. offered a good example with an ad campaign that shows women of a variety of ages and ethnic backgrounds side by side. The intergenerational and inclusive sense of community appeals to the Vibrant Woman's aspirations. She just wants to know that "women like me" are welcome at your bank, store, or airline.

2. Offer her all the information she needs to make an educated decision. Brand websites that offer Vibrant Women lots of professional information show respect for her intelligence and ability to make decisions and are most likely to win her business. A good example is Olay.com, whose family of brands is embraced by Boomer women. Don't offer the voice of an expert telling her what to do. She is interested in your expert solely because she is seeking the most reliable source for the information she needs to make her own decision. As we will demonstrate to you in chapter 3, it is imperative that you identify which marketing segment your target among Vibrant Women represents and how you find the message and means of delivery that is right for her.

3. Wherever possible, persuade her through other "women like me." As we mentioned earlier, VibrantNation.com conducted a spokesperson survey for the StriVectin line of skin-care products and found that women overwhelmingly wanted to hear about anti-aging skin care not from an expert, unless that expert was another Vibrant Woman they trusted and one whose own skin was worth emulating. Remember that for Vibrant Women, the most persuasive sale is always a referral. In fact, 88 percent of women 50+ we surveyed have told us that referrals from other women, including on-line testimonials from strangers on sites like tripadvisor.com or angieslist.com, were the second most important source after their own personal experience "pushing them over the edge" in making a final purchase decision.

4. Customize your message. We hear from too many brands that ask why they need a different message for Vibrant Women than they deliver to women in their 30s and 40s, especially since economies of scale make it so much easier to target them in the mainstream vehicles (whether web portals like Yahoo or print magazines) that reach all women. We find it odd that marketers rarely ask the same questions when they target other demographic niches such as the Hispanic or LGBT communities and are willing to invest in customized programs even when those demographic niches spend far less money than Vibrant Women. Granted, customizing your communications for Vibrant Women takes more work and requires using niche sites and platforms, but the good news is that there are a growing number of sites such as VibrantNation.com that focus specifically on Boomer women, and almost every site that targets Boomers generally gathers more Boomer women than men. Moreover, smart marketers are increasingly recognizing that every niche worth targeting is worth targeting precisely and in an authentic and intentional way. Such approaches are rewarded by Hispanics, African-Americans, gay and lesbian consumers…and Vibrant Women.

INTEGRATED MARKETING AND SOCIAL MEDIA

Too many brands think that social media means either building a microsite and inviting members of the public to call it home or setting up a fan page on Facebook and thinking that makes a community. Online marketing today means meaningful engagement on-line and usually revolves around real community, which can't be faked for any age, especially women 50+. It also requires using tailored formats based on your brand and the ways your customers want to be engaged.

One example of such a campaign comes from Carnival Cruise Lines, which found an unexpected celebrity in its own ranks, a popular cruise director named John Healds. In addition to its member-driven forums, Carnival's John Heald's blog has become one of Carnival's most popular marketing tools. Another example of meaningful engagement on-line is H&R Block, which deploys eighteen of its 10,000 tax professionals to help consumers on Yahoo Answers, a site more likely to be visited by Boomer women than Twitter.

The phenomenon that led Susan Boyle to sell millions of albums started with a Youtube video.

Your best integrated marketing tool may start small and may come from unexpected places. Youtube (owned by Google) works beautifully with the Vibrant Woman demographic, in the right circumstances. The phenomenon that led Susan Boyle to sell millions of albums started with a Youtube video, as did (on a smaller scale) the definitely low-key video of author Kelly Corrigan reading a chapter from her book *The Middle Place* to a group of visibly moved women. Corrigan's video has been viewed almost five million times and her book remained on *The New York Times* best-seller list for six months.

What do these examples teach us? First, successful social media marketing doesn't mean simply inserting content on Facebook, Twitter, or any other site. It means finding the right fit between content, medium, and audience. If you gain these things, there is no reason your campaign will not succeed with Vibrant Women. And, second, while no brand can ignore new media, don't waste time on sites or tools that don't enable you to deliver real benefits to consumers. (Do you really need Twitter? Or Facebook? Or would a more targeted site be the better vehicle for you?) When you find a social media tool that connects with your market, work it to the exclusion of others. The Internet can confuse marketers because anything seems possible. Your real goal should be finding the one or few things that work for you and then committing to them.

The Voices of Vibrant Nation

The changes associated with the Vibrant Woman lifestage can make it a challenge to staying connected to family and friends in the traditional ways. Carol is one among many who have found her community of support in the form of virtual strangers.

ON ONLINE COMMUNITY
BLOG BY CAROL ORSBORN, "INSIDE THE NATION"

Vibrant Women are highly motivated to go on-line as they discover the value and importance of networks of like-minded women offering support, information and connection.

Ever since I got my doctorate from Vanderbilt in ritual studies and adult development, I've made it my business to stay abreast of the latest thinking in academic circles about the science of resilience. One of the key factors influencing resilience that shows up consistently in the research is the individual's access to a community that offers support.

The irony for me was that hard upon my becoming a newly minted Ph.D. ten years ago, I moved from Nashville to the West Coast to be closer to my aging parents. Like the mystical village of Brigadoon, the friends, mentors, and support systems that had seen me through the challenges of pursuing a second-career degree quickly evaporated into the mists. Even before I was unpacked, I was consumed with care giving and then end-of-life issues related to both my parents at the same time as my children were leaving the nest. My husband offered great support, but one person—no matter how loving—does not a community make.

To make a long story short, a real community—one that gets you at your deepest levels, that makes you feel that you're not crazy or alone, that provides information and access to real resources—is not always that easy to find. In fact, I think many of us in the Vibrant Women 50+ crowd have gone through a long, dry spell. I'm talking about those of us who have moved from one place to another, who have lost the easy connections with other women in the same age and stage of life that we take for granted when our kids are still in the house, who have become estranged for any number of reasons from the organized communities that may have served us so well earlier in our lives.

To top it off, until Vibrant Nation came on the scene, we did not even have access to the kinds of vital on-line communities that were developing for other lifestage cohorts, like the mom and grandparenting sites. In fact, just ten years ago, most of our computers still functioned more as e-mail answering machines than as the vibrant networks of like-minded women offering the support, information, and reassurance to one another for which we yearned.

While many in the Vibrant Nation community undoubtedly have deep wellsprings of communal life from which to draw, both those of us who have been well-served as well as those of us who have been looking for something more, have something in common. We are discovering that there is not necessarily anything "virtual" about an on-line community for women at our own lifestage and experiences, such as the one we are building together at VibrantNation.com.

At a time in our lives when women traditionally become marginalized from the societal mainstream and isolated from one another, our revolutionary zeal has happily converged with technology to allow us to do what no generation of women in history has ever been able to achieve: grow both the breadth and depth of our social networks.

Make no mistake about it. The exponentially increasing vibrancy of our website—as it is revealing itself to us day-by-day—is changing the everyday reality of many, many women 50+. Look around everywhere, and you will see women talking about real things, useful things, fun things. They write things like "To know that I am not alone in this indescribable unsettled feeling is a great relief to me today." And "I just love VN and what it stands for and how we all can become friends and family on here."

You can read it for yourself, in post after post: at a stage in our life when previous generations became increasingly marginalized and powerless, we are, instead, becoming increasingly visible and resilient. This is not only a contribution we are making to one another but to the science of resilience.

ON DEEPENING THE CONVERSATION ONLINE
FROM A CONVERSATION ON VN

Subject: "I canceled my FB account after I found VN."

Storytaker:

After finding VN and reading the posts for several weeks, I canceled my Facebook page. Even though this is all Internet, women on VN share their dreams, fears, and their life stories. It doesn't begin to compare with the trivia on FB, in my opinion. When people are willing to open up and share who they are, people connect, friendships are made, and lives are changed- instead of just reading words.

Moongoddess:

I hardly ever check my fb anymore. Except for a few random friend postings and a few pictures, I don't get a lot out of it. However, I did see VN and decided to check it out.

Dynomomma:

I completely agree with Storytaker. I was also urged to join Facebook. After the first few days and some exploring, I got completely bored by the twitter type entries. No one ever said anything of any real meaning, no conversations. Some of the members asked to be my friend because we graduated from the same university only 20 years apart, absolutely nothing in common. I think she was trying to meet a certain number of friends. Finding some old friends wasn't even a thrill. So I canceled and joined VN and have loved it.

My advice:

Parents/grandparents have to do EVERYTHING they can to keep the lines of contact and communication open. It is just as much our responsibility to make the steps to keep contact. My grandson, now 5, can and does turn Skype on by himself and "beams" himself into grandma's house when he wants to. It is a delight to be in the other room and hear him call for grandma, and yes, I will go running (when I can...LOL) just to have a talk with him, even if it is about how he hurt his finger or how his little sister made him mad or even why mom or dad won't give him a second piece of cake. A month ago he was on Skype with me, and I heard his mom squeal in the background. I looked closer and got to see my granddaughter's first steps. If I lived across the street I might have missed that. I could miss many things living in the same town or city. With the technology of today, we can miss less now, no matter where we live.

ON LIKE-MINDED WOMEN FINDING EACH OTHER ON- AND OFF-LINE
FROM A CONVERSATION ON VN

Vibrant Women take off-line communities on-line, and vice versa.

Rebecca123:

Any Vibrant Nation-ers want to make a group for the November NaNoWriMo (National Novel Writing Month)? A reader response from my post about "releasing the writer/artist within," yakkity has suggested this opportunity to write, write, write for the month of November. Anyone interested in starting up a "home base" group of us fans of Vibrant Nation who love to write and want to challenge ourselves while encouraging each other? Hey, thanks again, yakkity!

Marsha:

I live in a suburb of Buffalo, NY. I would be very interested. Is anyone else in this area interested?

Rebecca123:

Hi, Marsha! There are writing groups thru NaNo (also called NaNoWriMo, for National Novel Writing Month) all over the world. Seemed like an especially large bunch of groups in New York, including Buffalo. Sign up on the site, and you can meet with your group in person there in Buffalo, and we can also be buddies on-line as a Vibrant Nation group, to encourage and pester each other. Sign up soon! The site is interesting (read the history) and easy to enroll for November. It's only held once per year for novel writing, so check in to it soon! I'm becca1 on NaNo, if you want to sign up as buddies!

SatorisWings:

I like the direction this discussion is taking. I really think our age group has a lot to offer, be it fiction, nonfiction, novels, short stories, magazine articles, whatever one wants to do. In days gone by, it was the old-time storytellers who gave direction, not by wagging their fingers and telling everyone they screwed up, but by telling stories with a not-so-obvious moral. They can be fun stories. They can be serious. They can be raunchy, or they can be religiously written. It doesn't matter. There is so much potential here with all of us, that it excites me. Let's all do something.

ON INCORPORATING ON-LINE COMMUNITIES INTO THEIR DAILY ROUTINES
FROM A CONVERSATION ON VN

Vibrant Women experience "withdrawal" if they can't access their favorite sites, and their desire to stay connected drives their mastery of technology.

Olga:

HELP! I'm in VN withdrawal!

I'm visiting my mother for a few days. She has no Internet access. As a result, I am limited to piggybacking on nearby unsecured networks. I can't always get a signal. I MISS YOU GUYS! Any suggestions for getting better signals from her home would be greatly appreciated. (Yes, I can go to the nearest Starbuck's, but there's only so much coffee I can drink-lol).

SeaWriter:

Hi Olga! Do you have a 3G phone? Maybe you could use that to get on-line while you're visiting your mother. If not, have a great visit. We'll miss your voice, though, so hurry back!

Olga:

No, but I'm gonna look in to it.

Dallas Lady:

Definitely, you need an iPhone~! Oh, it is cumbersome to use to post, but it is an avenue that works nonetheless.

Actually you need to get your mother Internet access and hook her up with VN too~~~~

I would love to have Olga's mom on here!

dynamomma

I have a laptop that I can do the same things on no matter where I am if I can get a cell phone signal. When we go somewhere and I know there is going to be something, like pay a bill, that needs to be done while we're gone, I'll take the laptop. It works for the essentials. It also works so that I don't have VN withdrawal! (smile)

ON GETTING A VIRTUAL HUG
FROM A CONVERSATION ON VN

The emotional connections *Vibrant Women* make on-line are real. They take the risk of sharing deeply, express their real feelings, take risks, and learn as they go: all the hallmarks of true community.

yakkity1:

Shame on me – "VN Hall of Stupidity" Thread

Please accept my humble apologies for my recent thread on which I expressed myself in a not-so-Vibrant manner. The subject was hitchhiking, and I was (and remain) more concerned with the driver's safety than with her satisfaction with doing what she felt to be the right thing.

She has every right to live her life as she sees fit, and my emotional response neither recognized nor respected that right, and for that I am sorry.

jeanniep:

You're the best, Yakkity1—such a kind, sincere person. We all get a little overly emotional about certain subjects.

granny in long johns:

How brave and sweet of you to recant on your post. I also wrote something rather negative today and had a spaz in a post. I felt obliged to write back to the VN members who put me back on a positive track. My

Indian friend has told me a good expression: A true friend will tell you when your face is dirty. I applaud your humility.

Olga:

Apology accepted. A truly Vibrant Woman knows when to apologize.

yakkity1:

If it were humanly possible, I'd be giving each of you a great big hug, just like this:

(((((my Vibrant Nation friends)))))

but with a line crossing out "Vibrant Nation." You ladies are my friends, period.

---

[1] Stephen Reily and Carol Orsborn, Ph.D., "Well-Connected and Wired," VibrantNation.com, March 18, 2009, http://www.vibrantnation.com/assets/1079/VN_White_Paper_Release.pdf. *This quantitative study was conducted from June 2-June 5, 2008, and consisted of a web-based survey of fourteen open- and closed-ended questions. In all, 1,000 U.S. women were interviewed, all aged 45 years or older, representing a cross section of marital status and with an annual household income of $75,000. Some 70% (701) of them were 50+. Of these, 50 percent reported a household income over $100,000. Quantitative data was supplemented by qualitative research undertaken by Vibrant Nation over the past two years as well as Dr. Carol Orsborn's original generational and adult development studies. The complete report is available on VibrantNation.com.*

[2] Brent Green, *Marketing to Leading-Edge Baby Boomers* (Ithaca, NY: Paramount Market Publishing, Inc., 2003).

[3] Stephen Reily, "Tech Survey: Boomer Women Are Early Adopters of New Consumer Electronics,"VibrantNation.com, February 17, 2010, http://www.vibrantnation.com/stephen-reily-flash -forward/2009/02/25/vibrantnation-com-tech-survey-boomer-women-are-early-adopters-of-new -consumer-electronics/.

[4] According to "AARP and the Center for the Digital Future," 42 percent of men and women 50+ check the Internet for news daily as compared to only 18 percent of those under 20;Tameke Kee, "Step Away from the Computer, Kids: Baby Boomers Embrace Social Media," MediaPost News, June 2008, http://www.mediapost.com/publications/?fa=Articles.showArticle&art_aid=85173.

3

THE MOTIVATIONAL MARKETING PYRAMID:

Segmentation and Stage

Social scientists as well as market researchers are just now realizing that a woman's life at 50+ is not a slow, sad decline into "old age," nor even a prolonged, static period of "maturity" or regret. It is, instead, a vibrant lifestage that arises from great changes and continues to advance through dynamic transitions.

As we discussed in the last chapter, Vibrant Women are the first generation of women in history whose social networks either remain stable or grow as they age. These women are motivated to tap into existing relationships and seek out new connections not just because they are socially oriented, but because their needs and interests change as they age. In fact, social scientists as well as market researchers are just now realizing that a woman's life at 50+ is not a slow, sad decline into "old age," nor even a prolonged, static period of "maturity" or regret. It is, instead, a vibrant lifestage that arises from great changes and continues to advance through dynamic transitions. The ramifications for marketers are multifold. For starters, the fact that women 50+ are growing as they age means that the demographic is not monolithic, presenting a unified face to the world. On the other hand, that growth does take place within a progression similar to developmental hierarchies at other stages of life. Happily for marketers, when it comes to discerning key motivational drivers, there is a distinct correlation between stage of growth and consumer segment. In fact, the more precisely marketers can pinpoint the segment of their particular target consumer, the more nuanced and powerful your motivational messaging will be.

There is a second, equally important ramification. Social scientists and market researchers have learned that it is in the transitions from one motivational stage to another that the individual is most open to making changes in her life. Whether it is the 13-year-old's teenaged angst, the 20-something's identity crisis, or the 50-year-old reinventing herself, it is in transitions to new stages that the consumer is most likely to question the status quo, rethink choices, and (of particular note to marketers) attach herself to new brands.

THE END OF ONE SIZE FITS ALL

The corresponding challenge for marketers is that the dynamic demographic is not a candidate for the "one-size-fits-all" marketing strategies and motivational messaging that may have appeared to do the trick in generations past. Regardless of her segment, however, one thing is certain: she is her own woman at her own, distinct lifestage. The ways she makes purchase decisions differ markedly from earlier stages in her own life, from previous generations at her age, and from younger women today.

In place of "one size fits all," the savvy marketer seeks to understand the distinct motivational drivers that define the Vibrant Woman marketplace. In our illuminating study of women 50+, we posed an open-ended question about the stages of life when the Vibrant Woman had changed her motivation for choosing certain brands over others. Almost every woman in the study reported that her motivations changed dramatically as she entered her late 40s and 50s. Moreover, this shift did not arise as many marketers had assumed it would—because she began saving more money or trading down as she approached retirement. The Vibrant Women we surveyed told us that it came, instead, from a variety of influences, including transitional lifestage events (living in an empty nest, losing a parent or spouse), physical changes (menopause, surviving breast cancer), new family roles (grandparent, caregiver), and social changes (travel and volunteer work that raise social and environmental awareness, for example). In fact, defying the stereotypes, Vibrant Women actually have greater financial stability than at any other time in their life, providing them with both the discretionary income and motivation to satisfy their own needs. Vibrant Women observe their lives changing as they enter a new stage of life, and the way they make purchase decisions changes with it. Based on this research, we present the first market segmentation of Vibrant Women, grounded in the motivational factors we have observed as they enter and transit this dynamic new stage of life.

THE FIVE SEGMENTS OF THE VIBRANT WOMAN CONSUMER MARKET

1. Values Endorsers

Approximately 14 percent of our study's Vibrant Women reported that they are now motivated to purchase brands that satisfy their interest in environmental/green values and social, health, and safety issues. Only 2 percent say that they were similarly motivated in their 20s. Experience and increasing wealth allows the Values Endorser to follow her beliefs (environmental, social, moral) in choosing where to spend her money. As one Values Endorser respondent said, "I've become freer to support manufacturers with social policies similar to mine, and I simply don't purchase goods if I can't find manufacturers that met my approval."

2. Simplicity Seekers

Some 20 percent of the Vibrant Women in our study told us that they seek, above all, value and simplicity in choosing one brand over another. These women are not just cost-cutters, although some are focusing on savings as they prepare for the future. They are primarily and increasingly selective, and uninterested in buying things they don't need, in buying things that won't last, or in paying more than necessary for the things they do need.

3. Self-Interested Spenders

Almost half of all Vibrant Women respondents – 48 percent – reported that they now make purchase decisions based on whether brands, products, and services acknowledge and meet their specific needs. This was not true at earlier lifestages. Fewer than 25 percent of them said that they made decisions for this reason in their 20s, and barely 30% of them said that it was true in their 30s. In the study, they reported that during these earlier decades of their lives, they consistently purchased the same brands either honoring brand loyalty or "ignoring their own needs." But as they aged, these women responded that they have become more selective, willing to shift loyalty to the brands that recognize and meet their needs. As one respondent said, "I decided to buy what interested me and—totally and irrevocably—to write off all those companies that weren't interested in seeking me as a consumer."

4. Experiential Indulgers

About 9 percent of Vibrant Women respondents reported that they make buying decisions based on their ability to enjoy new and expensive brands. More status-conscious than the other three segments, these consumers enjoy their ability to buy whatever they want and follow cultural leads in trying out the status-oriented brands they buy. As one respondent said, "Cost be damned, I want the best for my hubby and me."

5. Other Pleasers

Only 2 percent of Vibrant Women reported that they now make purchase decisions based on the needs of others. A full 15 percent reported that purchase decisions in their 20s were based on the needs of others; 9 percent report the same in their 30s.

These five distinct segments are interesting and useful in their own right. But when viewed through the lens of adult development theory, they reveal additional facets of relevance for marketers. Referring back to Abraham Maslow, we recall that the insightful psychologist postulated a hierarchy of human needs that form a basis for understanding how people mature through stages, with implications for marketers. Basically, Maslow's model of adult development was based on the pyramid, with the largest percentage of the population, the wide base of the triangle, consumed with survival issues. As life-sustaining issues are resolved over time, the individual becomes less reactive and gradually evolves toward a state of actualization at the peak of the pyramid, where altruism comes increasingly into play. Maslow put the percentage of people who achieve the highest stage of actualization at about 3 percent. We refer to our adaptation of Maslow's model to the Vibrant Woman marketplace as the Motivational Marketing Pyramid.

Aspirational Trends

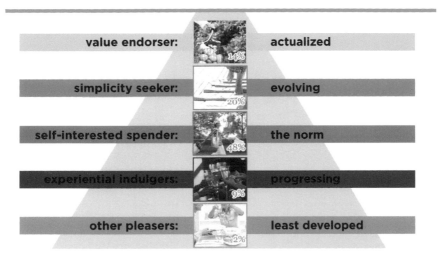

value endorser:	actualized
simplicity seeker:	evolving
self-interested spender:	the norm
experiential indulgers:	progressing
other pleasers:	least developed

MOTIVATED BY PURPOSE

The notion of progressing from a model of consumption motivated by survival to one motivated by purpose or meaning correlates to the five segments of the Vibrant Woman market, with one notable refinement. For Vibrant Women, the least evolved stages of adult development have virtually dropped off the bottom of the pyramid. Rather, the majority of women in our demographic have already moved through these earlier stages and are pressing upward toward actualization at a pace and rate that exceeds expectations.

For starters, let's take a look at the women in this demographic who are in the least developed stage of adult development, the "Other Pleasers." Other Pleasers represent the consumer segment of women whose sense of identity and survival depends on pleasing

Whether you call it rebellion, mid-life crisis, or reinvention, this woman casts aside her motivation to satisfy the needs of others.

others, whether partners, children, or other figures of authority. For these women, there is comfort and security in just wanting to be told what to do. Loyal to the status quo, they consistently put the needs of others ahead of their own.

Some marketers still believe that the majority of women 50+ still fall into this category. They portray the silver-haired matron serving dinner to the extended family, assure her that eight out of ten doctors recommend this or that product, and tell her that their bank will take care of her "like family." If these marketers are hoping to connect with the unprecedented wealth and influence of the Vibrant Woman, however, they will miss the heart of their generational target and capture less than 2 percent of the demographic.

In effect, the old "bottom" of the pyramid has become statistically irrelevant to the marketer. We now turn our attention to the second smallest consumer segment: Experiential Indulgers. As they make their way up the Motivational Marketing Pyramid and rebel against their previous conditioning, Other Pleasers evolve into Experiential Indulgers. Whether you call it rebellion, mid-life crisis, or reinvention, this woman casts aside her motivation to satisfy the needs of others. For instance, if she used to book family vacations at the Holiday Inn because her value-conscious mother always did, she now refuses to stay there for the very same reason: because her mother always did. Instead of worrying about pleasing her mother, she'll head for the Ritz-Carlton, winning lots of bragging points with her status-conscious peers. And sometimes, she'll even leave her children and husband behind, heading off with girlfriends for a weekend at the spa or even larger experiences, such as adventure expeditions and pampering cruises. While she experiences this stage as freedom, she is often unconsciously acting in knee-jerk reaction to her own past. She will deliberately seek destinations, products, and services, sometimes even regardless of value or effectiveness, simply to prove to the world that she is her own woman and a Vibrant Woman of means.

"I'VE WAITED LONG ENOUGH"

The woman in this segment is often aware—and sometimes even proud—that she is indulging herself: the flip side of putting others' needs before her own. In fact, she is the woman who wants what she wants when she wants it, as in the classic Botox ad where two friends lunching together hold up the protest signs: "This is my turn" and "I've waited long enough." Because of her larger-than-life stance, the Experiential Indulger is mistaken by some marketers to be the dominant consumer segment of the woman 50+ marketplace. Yet only 9 percent of the Vibrant Women in our study fit this profile, a larger segment than the Other Pleaser category but hardly the majority.

For that we must advance to the next consumer segment: the Self-Interested Spender. As you will recall, our research shows that this is

---

"I have disposable income but have started avoiding brands that ignore me."

---

the largest of all the segments, clocking in at a whopping 48 percent. So who is the Self-Interested Spender? She's the one who has progressed through the stage of knee-jerk reactivity to her original programming in order to make original, independent choices. She doesn't want to be taken care of (Other Pleaser) or manipulated by marketers into making expensive, trendy choices (Experiential Indulgers.)

Rather, she says things like: "I have disposable income but have started avoiding brands that ignore me" and "I reject brands that treat me like I'm a gullible, trend-slave 20-year old." If the marketer tries to appeal to this woman by telling her that "eight out of ten doctors recommend," she'll tune out your pitch. She'd rather get her information (on-line or off) from someone she can trust. And that trusted adviser? As she told us clearly in the same study: "Someone like me."

In our Ritz-Carlton example, she is the woman who goes on Facebook and notices that her friend recently went on a family trip,

---

She is free to pick and choose the "best-of" from all stages of her life, as well as incorporating new products, services, and behaviors.

---

staying at the Holiday Inn. Seeing the photos of the grandkids having a blast at the pool, she thinks to herself "Hmmmm. I haven't stayed at a Holiday Inn in ages. It would sure save us a bundle. Maybe we should give it a try." She may still go to the Ritz-Carlton for a romantic getaway with her husband or enjoy the spa and dining facilities on a special occasion weekend with her girlfriends. But no longer driven by reactivity to her own past, she is free to pick and choose the "best-of" from all stages of her life, as well as incorporating new products, services, and behaviors. She makes her decisions on the basis of the genuine value and utility of the purchase and is not making choices primarily to please others. But if she has made so much progress, where more does she have to grow?

MOVING UP THE PYRAMID

The answer is once again higher up on the Motivational Marketing Pyramid, to the next two segments of the Vibrant Woman marketplace. These are the segments we refer to as the Simplicity Seeker, comprising 20 percent of the demographic as a whole, and, at the Motivational Marketing Pyramid's peak of actualization:

She says things like: "I am putting quality over quantity".

Values Endorsers at 14 percent. As Maslow and others hypothesized, the upward trend is characterized by the progressive move from concerns about "me" to "other," not in the needy and childlike way this woman, at an earlier stage of her life, once put other's needs before her own. Rather, it is a move toward increasing altruism, where the good of the whole is not about protection of one's self, but rather of the willingness to defer gratification and make sacrifices in service of higher values such as meaning and purpose.

As independent as the Self-Interested Spender is, her considerations still center on what she wants, her own needs and interests. As she progresses from this stage toward the top of the pyramid, her personal needs and what is good for society increasingly converge. In the case of the Simplicity Seeker, this is the woman who seeks quality and simplicity to explore a more authentic life. She says things like: "I am putting quality over quantity" and "I'm making smarter decisions on brands and products that I need and that will last." Tell this woman that "you deserve it" or "more is better," and she will run the other direction. For her, aspirational advertising holds the promise of balance, simplicity, and a stress-free life.

THE PEAK OF MOTIVATIONAL DEVELOPMENT

And with this, we arrive finally at the peak of the pyramid. For the 14 percent who fit the profile of the Values Endorser, her primary motivation is no longer even about the convergence of what is good for her and for society. Rather, making values-based choices trumps all else. This is the woman who says: "I only buy what's

---

Any dramatic shift in a generation's brand-buying motivation creates new opportunities for marketers.

---

good for the environment and the world" and "I'm freer to support manufacturers with social policies similar to mine, and I simply don't purchase goods if I can't find manufacturers that meet my approval." To appeal to this segment, the smart marketer will make it clear that they do more than talk shared values—they embody them. We have now come full circle from brands who succeed with the promise "to take care of you" to brands who succeed by asking for and deserving her support.

While at 14 percent, this segment is at the top of the Vibrant Woman's Motivational Marketing Pyramid, it is a far heftier percentage than the 3 percent of actualized individuals at the peak that psychologist Maslow postulated when he first proposed his model of adult development. And while the top of the pyramid is, indeed, small by comparison to some of the other segments, it is, along with the Simplicity Seeker, the fastest-growing segment. We have already seen that the least-developed stages of development, Other Pleasers and Experiential Indulgers, have become statistically unimportant and that the Self-Interested Spender is now the majority of the demographic, comprising what we term a new base for the Motivational Marketing Pyramid. Assuming history holds true, we can expect that over time, this new base will also have had its day. For that reason, we advise marketers in search of aspirational messaging to look higher up the pyramid toward new levels of simplicity and altruism and away from icons drawn from the assumption that she spends money only to gain the approval of others.

IMPLICATIONS FOR MARKETERS

A ny dramatic shift in a generation's brand-buying motivation creates new opportunities for marketers. As we've noted, the changes that Vibrant Women undergo as they reach 50 are dramatic and reflect their new sense of freedom, personal preferences, and a strong sense of why they choose some brands over others. They are twice as likely to select brands based solely on their personal needs than they did in their 20s or 30s. Similarly, they are four times less likely to focus on the needs of others (husband, children, etc.) in their 50s and 60s as they were during their 20s. Finally, Vibrant Women are now more than six times as likely to make purchase decisions based on their personal values (environmental and/or social concerns) as they were in their 20s. With this knowledge in hand, marketers are equipped to engage these consumer segments in uniquely successful ways while avoiding turning other segments away.

Self-Interested Spenders make up almost half of Vibrant Women. While crafting a motivating message for her is not difficult, there are surprisingly few good examples of companies that actually do it. One successful example is Not Your Daughter's Jeans. The praise one VibrantNation.com blogger showered on this brand is featured in the Vibrant Voices section that follows, and it says a lot about how the physical construction of the brand's product serves Vibrant Women so well. But for our purposes here, we want to simply focus on the brand's name.

We once heard a marketer say that the name "Not Your Daughter's Jeans" was a bad idea because it reminded women that they were aging. She went on to remark that older women don't like admitting they can't still wear their daughter's jeans. This marketer missed the point. Self-Interested Spenders over 50 already know that they can't wear their daughter's jeans. They are prepared to

Vibrant Women are now more than six times as likely to make purchase decisions based on their personal values.

reward marketers who understand this fact of life without resorting to treating them condescendingly like stereotypical "grannies." In fact, the brand name itself winks at this Vibrant Woman with a wry, respectful sense of humor. To them, she is an insider, sharing with her the ironic understanding that a body at mid-life is different than her daughter's teen, 20-, or even 30-something physique. But it was this Vibrant Woman, after all, who constituted the first generation of women to transform jeans from a utility garment to a fashion statement. It is in her fashion DNA to understand that blue jeans need to fit well to be enjoyed. Not Your Daughter's Jeans captures the idea that the Vibrant Woman deserves her own jeans without sounding like she's old, and they do so in an upbeat, sexy manner that is reinforced by on-target print and on-line advertising.

Similarly to the designer jeans example, there are many other categories where women 50+ want to wear the same types of clothes as younger women but will appreciate not just customization in product but customization in name. Spanx revolutionized the girdle industry. Why can't underwear or leggings (slightly thicker and softer than that for younger women) be sexy without seeming cheap? Too many brands forget the Vibrant Woman's sense of humor. The "Not Your Daughter's" brand gives women the chance to laugh at the fact that their bodies have changed, but it does so in a way that also gives them the attention they deserve and welcome: recognition for being exactly as they are.

Simplicity Seekers spend money to simplify. As we noted above, marketers should not assume that the Simplicity Seeker does not want to spend money. In fact, her shift into this consumer segment can ironically spark enormous spending. As architect Sarah Susanka points out in her book *The Not So Big House*, she might buy or build a new and even more expensive home that meets her desire to live more intentionally, but smaller. She may replant her garden with a focus on low-maintenance plants. And her desire to shed and simplify her life can mean dozens of trips to the Container Store.

A focus on simplicity can also motivate the desire to travel, but with the locus of attention moved to experience, rejuvenation, or adventure, rather than on consumption for the sake of status or self-indulgence. The urge to simplify and its hand-in-hand thirst for meaning can also motivate the desire to explore her inner creativity, as organizers of writing programs and retreats have been delighted to discover.

The Simplicity Seeker is also buying new clothes, often seeking more expensive items as she focuses more on quality than quantity. One thing Vibrant Women appreciate about designer Eileen Fisher is that Fisher's designs and color palates don't change dramatically from year to year. Vibrant Women, who eschew trendiness in favor of stylish clothes that flatter their figures, reward designers who understand that they don't like the idea of a wholesale wardrobe change every year or two. Implying that women should throw good money at transitory fads feels like an insult to the Simplicity Seeker.

Values Endorsers spend money to help others. As with the Simplicity Seeker, the Values Endorser does not stop spending money just because she is motivated by a wider range of considerations. But marketers need to be sure to focus on her desire to spend money in ways that help others as much as they help her. One great example: TOMS Shoes has built its business with a campaign that promises "for every pair of shoes you purchase, TOMS will give a pair of shoes to a child in need." As one VibrantNation.com members said, "I'm stylin' and doing good at the same time."

The TOMs business model, which has even earned its own name (the "One for One" movement), reinforces how marketers should appeal to each Values Endorser's inner philanthropist. Her interest in travel, politics, and even shopping is intimately connected to her interest in giving back. Appealing to the inner philanthropist of the woman 50+ is not the same thing as "cause marketing"—a term that refers to companies that partner with nonprofits to encourage a connection in the mind of consumers between the for-profit and a cause they respect. Vibrant Women, and especially Values Endorsers, can be cynical about marketers' motivations, and just as they will reward those who engage her in real philanthropy, they will turn away from those who seem to adopt it only to open her wallet. And Vibrant Women can tell the difference.

We found another great example of how to engage the Values Endorser in travel planner (and Vibrant Woman) Janet Moore, who has led adventure travelers to exotic locations for almost thirty years. A few years ago, a coalition of women's colleges asked Janet to offer a tour for women only. They wanted a tour that shifted the focus from sight-seeing to connecting with women leaders in other countries to explore "issues that connect us all."

That trip quickly sold out, and twenty-nine women enjoyed a unique chance to visit South Africa and meet women leaders there. But the trip produced much more than memorable experiences.

Appealing to the inner philanthropist of the woman 50+ is not the same thing as "cause marketing."

After the trip, the travelers formed a steering committee to continue the conversations they had begun on the trip; created their own nonprofit, which has since funded two libraries in South Africa;

It didn't take long for this wired worker to realize that the same click of a mouse that allowed her access to resources, knowledge.

and rejoined for a series of tours (now called "Among Women: An International Dialogue") that recently returned from its third adventure—this time to India and Bangladesh. Why has this effort succeeded on so many levels? Because it recognized, first of all, the hunger among Vibrant Women in or aspiring to the Values Endorser segment to connect with each other, the energy that such connections generates, and the capacity to get Vibrant Women to use their money to change the world.

We should note that the segments of the Vibrant Woman marketplace influence one another and the aspirational draw, as we've indicated earlier, is top-down. Capturing Vibrant Women does not require speaking to each segment on its own, but neither should the marketer assume, as many do, that the majority of women 50+ are Other Pleasers or Experiential Indulgers, segments at the bottom of the pyramid who have become statistically irrelevant.

Rather, the savvy marketer recognizes that the Vibrant Woman knows she has entered and is transiting through a new lifestage and will reward you for recognizing her special needs and interests. This hunger for recognition applies to all Vibrant Women even as they progress through various stages up the Motivational Pyramid. Similarly, a message that ignores the changes she has undergone (and will continue undergoing) is the surest way to turn her off. She is not her daughter, and she knows she shouldn't be wearing her daughter's jeans.

On this promising note, we conclude part 1 of *Vibrant Nation*. In part 2, Flash Forward, we take a deep dive into the real world of Vibrant Women and what they are thinking, doing, buying, and dreaming about at this dynamic stage of their lives. In keeping with our findings, we center the target of our considerations on women in the dominant consumer segment and up on the Motivational Marketing Pyramid: Self-Interested Spenders, Simplicity Seekers, and Values Endorsers. In this way, we get to know not only the largest segment of the women 50+ marketplace in depth, but the aspirations that are driving them through this dynamic period of their lives.

The Voices of Vibrant Nation

Vibrant Women progressing upward on the Motivational Marketing Pyramid find opportunity even in change and chaos.

ON CHAOS AND OPPORTUNITY
BLOG BY CAROL ORSBORN, "INSIDE THE NATION"

One of the benefits of turning 50+ is having expanded internal resources to call upon, especially when times are challenging. This is a quality many Vibrant Women are bringing not only to their personal issues, but to larger communal concerns.

I was seated in a circle of my friends, one-by-one bemoaning the state of the world. The all-too-familiar "hell in a hand basket" rant went something like this: "Health Insurance Reform," to which we all responded "Oy." "Greed on Wall Street." "Oy." "Tiger Woods." "Oy." "Unemployment, terrorism, global warming." "Oy, oy, oy."

Despite the fact that we were seated beneath fluorescent lights, it was as if the room had suddenly gone dim. Then it was the turn for the eldest and wisest amongst us to speak.

"Don't you get it?" she said. "An opportunity like this happens only two or three times a millennia—and we're here and this is it!"

Sandra was talking about no less than chaos—the creative opportunities inherent in the breakdown of the status quo.

The women in the circle instinctively understood what our friend was telling us. You don't get to be 50 or 60 without something pretty big breaking down somewhere along the way. I looked around the circle. Here was one who had survived a divorce, another who was dealing with serious illness, several whose adult children were in trouble.

And yet, I saw only the beloved faces of my friends who have learned through our life experiences that we can become strong enough to face whatever our situations may be with renewed perspective and creativity. Having developed the capacity over time to dig deep, we find it possible to hope for something unexpected, something important, something miraculous even when the facts of our lives seem to indicate otherwise.

When it comes to our personal lives, we have come to embrace chaos not as an imperfection in the universe, but as part of the natural order. We Vibrant Women who have journeyed to the forest many times know that when fire rages, there is not only destruction. For, too, it is the heat of the flame that breaks open the pinecone to release its seed. We have come to appreciate not only the broad green canopy above, but the broken tree limbs and blackened stumps stricken by lightening beneath our feet. These, we have learned, are not imperfections in the forest, but the forest, itself.

Now Sandra was challenging us to bring that same spirit we've honed through personal life experience to the world.

I am reminded of a favorite story of mine, shared in the 1950s by anthropologist Margaret Mead about the role of the postmenopausal red-tailed deer. Margaret explained that in their advanced years, it was the females who carried the wisdom of the pack.

"In times of drought, these old does could remember where once, long ago, under similar circumstances, water sources had been found. When spring came late, they recalled sunny slopes where the snows melted early. They knew how to find shelter, places where blizzards could be waited out. Under such circumstances, they took over the leadership of the herd."

And so it is that the five of us in the circle made a pledge, and I would ask you to join us, too. We have charged ourselves with the sacred mission of reframing our response to these challenging times. Instead of dimming the lights against the chaos, we must show the way to burning brighter still. We must point the way to where hope may yet be found. We must take a stand for the miraculous.

What we have already learned to do for ourselves, we must now do for the world.

Clearly, what motivates Vibrant Women now is different than what motivated them at a younger age. They are also richly aware that life is, and will continue to be, a long process of growth. As Sue says: "Life really does get better with age."

ON PROGRESSING THROUGH DIFFERENT LIFESTAGES
POSTCARDS TO OUR YOUNGER SELVES

We invite all Vibrant Nation members to write a "postcard to my younger self." What they write usually offers a useful (and often moving) contrast between where the Vibrant Woman was thirty years ago and where she finds herself now.

phyllis the ISSI lady:
Dear Phyllis, Wish you were here—Oh right, you will be. Listen. Time goes much faster than you think it will. Prepare well. Have fun but plan ahead. Put aside more money and keep your education going. There will be more changes in the world than in any other era in history. Get ready—and remember: Get out of the stock market the minute it hits 14,000 and stay out. Oh yeah—if you do end up with a lot of money to invest, stay far away from Bernie Madoff, Shearson Brothers, General Motors, and Chrysler. No, I'm not kidding. New words to learn—Google, Yahoo, Ebay, texting, twittering, and no I am not talking baby talk.
Bekah:
Label anything you put in storage.
gail maria:
Dear Younger Self: Why, why, why didn't you think about a career back in high school? Husbands aren't careers, except in my case, but it was a really

ill-conceived idea. They're hasta la bye-bye and you are left with an English degree. Btw, there was no upside to being so conciliatory in the settlements. Bad girl. They're rich and you're anxious....Planning girlie. Next time forget the Cinderella story and remember the Little Match Girl.

Heather C.:

All is forgiven. Come home.

Sue:

See, Mom was right! Life really does get a lot better with age.

Wise Weight Woman:

Dear Younger Self,

When they call you 'Patty Fatty' it doesn't mean you are fat. It means they think you are precious, cute, and adorable. When they tell you that you look like Aunt Ida, it doesn't mean you're fat like her. It means your face looks like her face. If you don't think you are fat, you won't create a fat body.

From Sentinela, the watcher in your soul

Susan M.:

Never forget to have fun! Go out and play. Try new things. Be brave in finding joy, not just in facing adversity. It will serve you well.

JustcallmeJudy:

Do not give up free nookie to anybody! If he doesn't make your knees knock together, don't sleep with him! Do it for you, not for him! BTW, look around for a chubby soul singer named Jessie and meet him twenty years earlier than you did! If you see a tall, handsome dude ranch employee who looks like your childhood lust object, Burt Lancaster, run like hell!

Smese:

Don't throw your pearls before pigs. It's a waste of good pearls, and it pisses off the pig.

joanie16350:

Even though the world started long before you got here and will go on long after, MAKE YOUR MARK ON IT.

GISMAMA:

Always remember "And it came to pass"; it didn't come to stay. Your childhood is preparing you for some really hard trials in the future, but YOU CAN DO IT ONE "BITE" AT A TIME. Think of eating the elephant and handle what you can, take a break and read a silly book, then handle some more. There is nothing you can't do or achieve. Hang in there, persevere, and get your college education. Always smile and eventually you will have something to smile about. Not everything makes sense when it's happening, but when you look back, you will find that it all is for your own good and it will make you stronger and better. Above all else, find that silver lining in every dark cloud. It's always there, although it may be hard to find sometimes. You are strong.

ON GROWING THROUGH CRISIS
A VN PROFILE

Vibrant Women have grown stronger because of the challenges they've faced in their lives. They are flexible and resilient, plus they know how to have a good laugh.

my member name: laurabuggg

where I live now: South Carolina

How did you get to where you are now?

A series of strange, sometimes frightening, sometimes wonderful occurrences

How do you see yourself differently now than you did ten years ago?

I am much more flexible and capable than I was at 41. I am wiser as well as more insightful. I like myself more.

Where do you see yourself in ten years?

I see myself surrounded by friends and family in a place that I own. Still singing, dancing, cooking, writing, painting, and dreaming.

a postcard to my younger self

Dear younger Laura,

I miss you a bit, but I'm thrilled you're not here because as much as I love you...you couldn't handle it.

Love Laura in the Now

ON CONNECTING WITH THE SELF-INTERESTED SPENDER
BLOG BY JUDI50+, "A BOOMER'S LIFE AFTER 50"

"I took my white jeans home. And when I tried them on again in my walk-in closet and looked in the mirror (I have a full-length mirror in my walk-in closet), I realized that the reason they made my tummy look so small was because they are a special brand of jeans...I found the jeans made especially for baby Boomer women."

I finally found a pair of white jeans at Lord & Taylor. The best part was that there was only one pair left on the rack and they were my size; the second best was that the jeans fit me to a tee; the third best was that the jeans were on sale; and the fourth best was that I had a 20-percent discount coupon on top of the sale.

No they didn't pay me to take the jeans out of the store...but it almost felt like they did....

Soooo, I took my white jeans home. And when I tried them on again in my walk-in closet and looked in the mirror (I have a full-length mirror in my walk-in closet), I realized that the reason they made my tummy look so small was because they are a special brand of jeans. Yes, I found the jeans I had read about over a year ago in People Style Watch magazine. I found the jeans made especially for baby Boomer women.

My new white jeans are made by the Not Your Daughter's Jeans Company (NYDJ). No wonder I like these jeans. I've tried on many, many brands of jeans that my daughter wears, and they never fit me. They are either too tight, too low cut, too wide, or too long (my new white jeans were too long too, but they needed only a little hem, not 10 inches taken off like some of the popular brands that my 20-something daughter wears).

According to the NYDJ label attached to my jeans, "NYDJ cannot be held responsible for any positive consequence that may arise due to my fabulous appearance when wearing my Tummy Tuck Jean," says Lisa Rudes-Sandel, the founder of this fabulous jean company. "You can thank me later," adds Lisa.

Lisa is right. I did have positive consequences with my white jeans. It happened two days after I purchased my NYDJ white jeans. It happened when I was having my jeans hemmed at the cleaners on Friday. I was standing tall in my NYDJ jeans as the tailor measured the hem. Another Boomer woman came into the store to pick up her cleaning and turned to see me in my jeans. "What fabulous white jeans," she said, "they fit you great, where did you get them?' "Thank you, thank you," I replied as I smiled, "Lord & Taylor on sale."

According to NYDJ, their jeans with the "Flatten Your Tummy" double "criss-cross" feature also lift my buttocks and allow me to look and feel one size smaller. (I am a size 4, so the one size smaller isn't the biggest benefit, but the buttocks lift is a definite plus.) Thank you, Lisa, your jeans are the best.

I think I will have to purchase another pair of these jeans in blue denim and maybe black denim too (I do need new jeans for casual jean Fridays at work). I read on the NYDJ website that these jeans are top sellers at nordstrom.com. I know where I'm headed the next time I want a new pair of jeans for the fall.

ON ASPIRING TO SIMPLICITY
BLOG BY SARAH GAYLE CARTER, "SARAH GAYLE CARTER'S JOURNAL"

"All of a sudden I had a light bulb go off in my head, a sort of epiphany of simplicity. It was almost as if all the pieces had been there for some time, but suddenly they all just kind of came together like a kaleidoscope. Chaos, chaos, chaos—and then one little turn and all the pieces fell together. In that instant, I knew that I wanted what my friends had: I wanted simplicity."

Let me start by telling you where I am now.

My name is Sarah Gayle Carter. Ten years ago, I had my own design business. I designed custom rugs, furniture, and other home furnishings. Today, I'm an artist—a painter. I've essentially left my life as a designer behind, and instead I paint landscapes and dog portraits. Yes, you read that right: I paint dogs. And I actually believe I can support myself on a modest-scale painting. The most interesting thing about this, for me, is that this is what I want. I'm perfectly happy, not just conceding. Isn't that something?

The story of how I got here is a long one, and kind of circuitous. I'll probably end up telling that story in multiple parts, over several entries in this journal. But for now I think I'll share how I came to feel that this slower, simpler life is right for me, for where I am right now.

One of the biggest turning points in my journey was a visit I made to Lexington last year. I made friends with a couple, both artists. She's a painter. He's a sculptor. They live in a house that looks like a shoebox on a concrete slab on the side of a mountain. They heat their house with a wood stove and grow a lot of their own food. They barter for what they need. And they're happy as clams. Understand that these are educated people who came from the same background I did, who have made a conscious decision to live their lives in a very different way from the path I've taken all my life. They wanted their work to be their art, and they were willing to make whatever accommodations were necessary for that to happen.

I don't know how I would have responded if I had met these friends ten years earlier, but for some reason, meeting them at this point in my life, my immediate response was to say, "Listen. You've got to tell me how much cash it takes to live like this." And I learned that my friends live on about $12,000 a year. They don't have health insurance. They don't have a cell phone or cable TV, and they drive old cars, which, for most people, would not be OK. But they are fine with their life. They wake up every day happy because they are doing what they love. I had never even considered this possibility before—but suddenly there it was, right in front of me.

All of a sudden I had a light bulb go off in my head, a sort of epiphany of simplicity. It was almost as if all the pieces had been there for some time, but suddenly they all just kind of came together like a kaleidoscope. Chaos, chaos, chaos—and then one little turn and all the pieces fell together. In that instant, I knew that I wanted what my friends had: I wanted simplicity. I realized that life is not just about all the running around that I had been doing for so long. I thought about all the frantic energy, the panic, the deadlines, always trying for more, more, more. Don't get me wrong. Building my business from nothing and sustaining it for ten years had been incredibly rewarding. I had a deep sense of accomplishment and had learned things about myself that I might otherwise never have known. But it had always been like having a tiger by the tail.

Now, looking at my friends and the different kind of life they had created for themselves, I realized that there is a sort of elegance in paring your life down to that sort of simplicity. It tied right in to other things that had been happening in my life for years. I thought, "I don't want to have to dance so fast that there's no time in the day to sit and read a book or call a friend or take a trip or, you know, live—and just be." I think I had been moving toward this epiphany for some time without knowing it. But now, finally, a lot of threads had come together, and I was standing on the threshold of something completely new.

[1]Stephen Reily and Carol Orsborn, Ph.D.,, "Well-Connected and Wired," VibrantNation.com, March 18, 2009, http://www.vibrantnation.com/assets/1079/VN_White_Paper_Release.pdf.
[2]Susanka, Sarah, *The Not So Big House* (Newtown, Connecticut: Taunton Press, 2000).

PART TWO

Flash Forward:
Exploring the Vibrant Woman's World

4

DEEP FASHION, BEAUTY, ANTI-AGING...

and the Meaning of Life

Regardless of what starts a conversation about fashion, fitness and beauty— whether or not it's okay to wear leggings at 60, or how much to spend on moisturizer—virtually every exchange ends up with women either questioning or affirming the meaning of life.

W hen Vibrant Nation was approached by a leading pantyhose company for advice about marketing to women 50+, we asked to see their advertisements and catalogs. They showed us page after page of teenagers and 20-somethings doing chorus-line kicks and somersaults flaunting their new line. The irony is that this company already recognized that their primary customer was a Boomer woman. But when we pointed out the discrepancy between the ages of their models and the targeted consumer, they were dumbfounded.

"But don't women 50+ want to be aspirational?" the chief marketing officer replied.

Of course, women 50+ have aspirations, especially when it comes to style, fashion, beauty, and fitness. But they don't aspire to look like their daughters or granddaughters. Rather, they aspire to be the best 50- or 60-year-old they can be. And that's saying a lot. With the likes of Sophia Loren, Madonna, Helen Mirren, Kim Cattrall, Sela Ward, Susan Sarandon, Sigourney Weaver, Meryl Streep, and even 60-year-old model Twiggy (launching her own Twiggy London line) as role models, women's expectations regarding what it means to look good at 50+ have come a long way. In many ways, the 2010 Academy Awards was a landmark year for Boomer women, who not only cleaned up across the spectrum of categories for talent and skill but turned heads of all ages for their red-carpet looks.

Clearly, Vibrant Women are putting a lot of thought and energy into their physical appearance. At the same age that Whistler's mother took to her rocking chair and our own mothers hid behind house dresses and muumuus, she's showing up for yoga and Pilates and spending money on facials, manicures, and a wide array of other offerings for fitness, beauty, fashion, style, weight loss, and more. But while she has a far more fit and youthful demeanor than her mother at the same age, the Vibrant Boomer Woman will be the first to tell you that she is still a work in progress. In fact, beneath her hip new haircut and spring wardrobe, you are likely to encounter

---

"How can I regain mastery over a body that has spun out of my control?"

---

unexpected reservoirs of uncertainty and ambivalence about the tensions between anti-aging and self-acceptance, style versus comfort, and organic approaches versus artificial enhancements and elective procedures. These are not issues easily resolved by the assurances or opinions of even the best sales clerk, beautician, or expert, even if such professional guides were readily available (which they assuredly are not.) Rather, they go to the very core of who this woman is becoming as she engages in her own less-than-placid journey between lifestages and levels of adult development in the Motivational Marketing Pyramid.

THE ROOT QUESTION

Regardless of how she expresses it, there is a root question contributing mightily to the tension she feels: "How can I regain mastery over a body that has spun out of my control?" Whether she asks this question consciously or unconsciously, it holds both poignancy and an element of surprise for a Vibrant Woman so used to calling the shots in her life. No matter what else she has accomplished—breaking the glass ceiling, raising a family, building a network that extended her influence in many realms—she now encounters physical attributes and challenges she cannot conquer.

Whether it's an extra layer of belly fat that no amount of diet or exercise can minimize, the first age spots on her still-strong hands, or the wrinkles that accompany her hard-won wisdom, she is forced to contemplate her ultimate powerlessness in the face of mortality. We have found at VibrantNation.com that regardless of what starts a conversation about fashion, fitness, and beauty —whether or not it's OK to wear leggings at 60 or how much to spend on moisturizer—virtually every such exchange ends up with women either questioning or affirming the meaning of life.

The connection between fashion, beauty, and philosophical stances is nothing new for this woman. Since Boomers first broke through the ladies-who-lunch aesthetic of white gloves and pointy bras that held sway through the early 1960s, they have brought thoughtful, alternative values to how they dress and treat their bodies. In the 1970s, the first round of Boomers borrowed from every ethnicity, geography, and fantasy they could conjure up, as long as it was comfortable to wear. They wore minimal makeup and refused to squeeze into their mothers' girdles, nylons, and slips. The original recyclers, they opened vintage stores, mixed-and-matched clothes, wore misshaped hats and neckties like Diane Keaton in

---

They wore minimal makeup and refused to squeeze into their mothers' girdles, nylons, and slips.

Annie Hall and/or leggings and leotards like Jane Fonda in her best-selling exercise videos. On 20- and 30-year-old bodies, all those looks worked.

A younger round of Boomers tempered the tendency toward rebelliousness but still negotiated doing fashion their own way through the decades of changing workplaces and maturing roles in life. In the 1980s, they wore power suits and ribboned blouses to reflect the new glass ceilings they were targeting, then adopted high heels and revealing clothes to show the world that yoga and Pilates had maintained the posture and taut limbs of youth.

But then the Vibrant Woman hit a wall. Eyes and attention from designers, retailers, and the beauty industry turned to younger women. And despite her best efforts, she was dealing with changes in her body and appearance that she could not reverse. She found herself increasingly worried whether she would ever again look as good as she felt. With precious little help from marketers, Boomer women have been largely on their own in addressing these questions, whether regarding what to wear on a casual day at work or whether to wear pantyhose or a spray tan to their daughter's wedding.

LOSING FAITH IN BRICK-AND-MORTAR

Retailers have not helped matters any. Most Vibrant Women actively dislike buying clothes and cosmetics in brick-and-mortar stores. The key reason: they can't find retailers they can count on to understand their tastes and preferences, both in the offerings on display as well as the shopping experience over all. When they do find a sympathetic retail brand, it is often a temporary situation

---

Vibrant Women also seek more privacy than many stores offer.

---

before a new crop of strategic marketers abandon "older women," however loyal, to rejoin the hunt for younger buyers.

Vibrant Women also seek more privacy than many stores offer. Moreover, they are sick and tired of being ignored by salespeople who don't understand how much money they have to spend. In fact, in a spring 2010 survey, a resounding 84 percent of

It is shocking to see so little innovation in targeting the faster-growing, richer population of women 50+.

VibrantNation.com members told us that clothing salespeople fail to meet their expectations. For all these reasons and more, Vibrant Women no longer enjoy shopping either as a hobby or as a solution-driven expedition.

When you listen to Boomer women long enough, you realize that no fashion brand or retailer is doing even some of what it could to capture their loyalty and, of course, their money. Even the ones who do can't seem to stick with it. In 2010, we saw Eileen Fisher abandon her loyal Boomer female base in a race for younger consumers. Talbots, despite a reputation for serving the needs of Vibrant Women, also seems to be increasingly ignoring its built-in growth market in favor of chasing a younger generation. These strategies make even less sense given the large number of Vibrant Women who name both Fisher and Talbots as brands that get them right (or at least, used to).[1]

Considering the number of new entrants in fashion offerings for women under 50, it is shocking to see so little innovation in targeting the faster-growing, richer population of women 50+.

ENGAGE HER ON-LINE. AND INNOVATE

During the same ten- to fifteen-year period when Boomer women were losing their faith in brick-and-mortar retail, the Internet exploded as a place that could serve their needs without many of the frustrations. The Internet is now the fastest-growing and most important venue for women's clothing and cosmetics purchases. Two out of three Vibrant Women are buying clothes on-line (15percent buy clothing only on-line), and Vibrant Women buy more cosmetics on-line than in department stores.[2]

The Vibrant Woman knows what she wants— she just isn't sure how to get it, where to get it.

One of the great pluses for marketers in the move from the brick-and-mortar to virtual world is that innovation on-line is a lot cheaper than new print campaigns. Additionally, marketers can follow the lead of real-time success stories. And there are plenty pointing the way, such as Zappos.com, who have hit the bull's-eye selling high-priced Taryn Rose shoes beloved by women 50+, among other popular brands. Herroom.com has succeeded by offering underwear and lingerie rated on the site by customers who share information with one another about which styles, sizes, and brands work best with their particular body types. LLBean.com provides filtering tools that guide its key customers, women at mid-life and beyond, to exactly the right coat at the right price, taking into consideration such factors as wind chill and moisture, with a few elegant clicks of the mouse. And of course ebay.com has become the equivalent of the 50+ woman's department store, one-stop shopping that allows her to find just what she knows she already wants. As we've noted, women are already buying a lot of cosmetics on-line at sites like Sephora.com, Fragrancenet.com, and QVC.com, in part because the prices are better but also because they can get more information there than anywhere else.

WHAT SHE WANTS

When it comes to fashion, fitness, and beauty, the Vibrant Woman knows what she wants—she just isn't sure how to get it, where to get it, and whether anybody in the fashion or beauty industry cares. What she wants is "to look good" or, at the very least, to not make a fool of herself. Asked "When shopping for clothes, what is the most important factor for you?" nearly three times as many (63 percent) in a Vibrant Nation survey chose "How it looks on" over "How it feels."[3] Of course, the Vibrant Woman wants it all—fits that flatter as well as comfort…and she's not so sure why she has to choose. In fact, where she once prided herself on breaking the fashion rules, she is now equally dedicated to beating the system. Resourceful and willing to make an investment, the Vibrant Woman is hungry for innovative solutions that will give her an increased sense of mastery over her looks. Tell her about a new brand of jeans that tames her belly fat without puckers or darts or show her a sexy nightgown that will use cutting-edge technology to wick away her hot flash, and she will be the first to seek them out. Add in that her purchase will make her healthier—improve the circulation in her legs or allow her neck to breathe—or that the cloth is made from organic bamboo and is good for the environment, and you've found the secret to untying her purse strings.

In her quest to look good, these issues are even more pronounced when it comes to beauty regimens and cosmetics. While she does not want to look like her daughter or granddaughter, her level of self-acceptance only goes so far when it comes to wrinkles, sagging skin, or thinning hair. In keeping with the complexity she exhibits in a host of categories, this woman declares herself free from society's youth-centric standards and expectations while at the same time driving the market for anti-aging products, services, and procedures. Equally important to her are the health promises and issues that come coupled with everything from the vitamins she puts into her body to the moisturizer she puts on her face. She goes to great lengths to read the fine print on the label, studying both benefits and warnings; 60 percent of those we surveyed are willing to pay more for products containing quality ingredients. More than half of these pay more for hypoallergenic products and antioxidants. What she can't find on the label or packaging material she will seek out on-line either from the brand's website or from her number one referral source: "women like me."

SERIOUS BUSINESS

Identifying and evaluating the best resources for fitness, fashion, and beauty is not a hobby for the Vibrant Woman. It's part passion and part survival, as she continues the ongoing process of defining who she is becoming as she ages. Still active at work and in her community, she does not have the luxury of taking refuge in invisibility. Both workplace and marketplace are judging her appearance daily. Every new physical challenge and every major meeting or event remind her that she is on the largely unmapped terrain of what it means to be an attractive Vibrant Woman at 50 and beyond.

Despite her determination to beat the system, she is hungry for attention and eager for the right kind of guidance. In fact, she is both indignant and mortified by how hard it is to find just about anyone in the fashion, fitness, and beauty industries who will take her seriously. Despite the odds, the women of Vibrant Nation are resolved to look and feel their best. And savvy marketers who make the attempt to help these women close the gap will be amply rewarded by her.

IMPLICATIONS FOR MARKETERS

When it comes to fashion and beauty, the Vibrant Woman's desire to be recognized by brands is increasingly bundled with her distrust of marketers who condescend to offer her empty praise or patronizing advice. Based on what Vibrant Women tell us, and what we observe in their behavior, here is an outline of tactics that will reward your investment in her.

> **Market to her through "Women like Me."** When it comes to fashion and beauty, as in categories and industries across the board, the best marketing tool for Vibrant Women is word-of-mouth. When considering spokespeople and experts, keep in mind that women want to know that the source offering advice or inspiration is someone from both the gender and lifestage who has personally advanced through the same lifestages and transitions, women who know the good and bad sides of aging, whether they happen to be a celebrity or not. This applies to designers, retailers, and entrepreneurs, as well. Women didn't just buy Eileen Fisher's clothing because they like its fit; they know that there is a real Eileen Fisher and that she herself is 50+ (which is why they feel not only confused but betrayed to see Eileen Fisher ignore its core audience of Vibrant Women).

> **Keep in mind that she doesn't aspire to be ignored.** Vibrant Women aspire to be all kinds of things, but 35 is not generally one of them. On the other hand, Vibrant Women don't demand that ads feature only women 50+. What they don't like is ads that never feature women 50+.

> **Show her you respect her by providing her with the facts.** Women loved Dove's globally viral "Evolution" video, which showed one face's transition from beautiful and natural to the artificial and air-brushed image in an ad. They admire the messaging behind Dove's line of "Pro-Age" cosmetics. But Dove's approach has motivated more conversations than cosmetics sales. Contrast this to the performance of Olay, which has built on its massive Regenerist platform to deliver increasingly segmented offerings such as Total Effects and Pro X in the anti-aging cosmetics field. Olay has not done this with clever imagery but rather with an abundance of useful information, presenting straightforward facts about their products together with extensive reviews and ratings from other women. The result is that women feel respected and

understood, empowered to make their own decision regarding which Olay products would work best for them. As a result, Olay dominates this space.

> **Make sure your compliments aren't rubbing her the wrong way.** The Vibrant Woman will bristle if you use words like "still" (as in, "you're still going strong") or words that come off as condescending. We put words like "fab" and "well-preserved" in that category, because they imply that the woman is only doing well "for her age." Instead, tell her that she can be "ageless," that she can look "as great as she feels," and always consider using humor to capture her contradictory desire to enjoy even what she can't control.

> **Engage her on-line.** The closer you can influence a consumer to her point of purchase, the better, so marketers need to be spending more time and resources reaching female fashion and cosmetics buyers on-line. Marketers should also develop their own e-commerce offerings in ways that work for Boomer women. The Internet offers (1) valuable content and (2) the opportunity to buy products; but too few brands or sites bring the two together. Companies that offer just one or the other should rethink their strategy. Visitors to e-commerce sites spend more time there if they are offered valuable content, and content-providing websites can build revenue models from e-commerce offerings.

The Vibrant Woman is determined and resourceful. Newly confronting wrinkles she can reduce but not erase, hair and eyebrows that are getting thinner by the day, and a body that is changing shape on her, she is once again a pioneer on uncharted territory, doing her best to figure it out as she goes. Help her solve her fashion and beauty problems, and treat her with respect, and the Vibrant Woman will find her way to you.

The Voices of Vibrant Nation

Vibrant Women embrace not only a broader but deeper definition of the role fashion and beauty have come to play in their lives.

ON EMBRACING THE PARADOX OF BEAUTY
BLOG BY CAROL ORSBORN, "INSIDE THE NATION"

Women 50+ have a complex relationship with aging and beauty. Those who allow self-acceptance and the desire to look as vibrant as possible to co-exist, have the potential to transform the tension of dichotomy into meaning.

The women of Vibrant Nation are resolved to look and feel our best. It doesn't take long, however, to realize that our members embrace not only a broader but deeper definition of the role fashion and beauty have come to play in our lives.

I realized this early on, when I asked for a recommendation for a moisturizer and found myself instead engaged in a conversation about whether to accept or fight signs of aging. I still wanted the recommendation of a moisturizer, by the way, but I appreciated the refreshing dimensionality and level of dialogue with peers I trusted. Trust me, this was not a conversation I was ever going to have with the girl wearing black lipstick behind the Lancome counter.

There is, in fact, a kind of ease and graciousness that has grown along with our membership, as we seamlessly segue between ballerina flats and the meaning of life. A great example of this is found in the conversation: "A good look for 2010" initiated by KMC. If you think tension or dichotomy, you'll get whiplash from following this thread. Think expanding to embrace the whole of what it means to be a Vibrant Woman 50+, and you'll get a much better read on what it means to be in the VN zone.

The thread begins with me and Catharine talking about things like belt buckles and dress coats made of boiled wool. SeaWriter meets us with the revelation of her lifelong collection of Hermes scarves, then raises us one with her retention of a personal trainer "that takes a holistic approach to fitness and energy."

Now Catharine is off of boiled wool and onto meditation, but it's only a couple of comments later before we're onto Olga's "good underwear is a must."

By the time we've made it through the first thirteen comments or so, we've touched on finding love, losing weight, and, yes, the meaning of life.

Writes Matriarch: "I really feel women need to concentrate less on what society says we should look like, and love self enough to wear what we want." And Olga (who if you recall last piped in about the importance of good underwear) replies: "It's not about conforming to society's expectations, but about saying, 'I like myself enough to take care of my physical appearance as well as my inner self.'"

Wow! Think about it.

Then we're off again, onto new hairdos and blending jeans with heels. See what I mean?

There was a time when I thought I would have to pick a team—care about my appearance or care about things "that really matter." Not any more. The VN zone is large enough to embrace it all, as together, we create a new definition of fashion and beauty that includes everything we are and can be, including the paradox.

ON LOOKING HER AGE
FROM A CONVERSATION ON VN

The Vibrant Woman wants retailers who understand that she aspires to look the best she can at her own age, not her daughter's.

Former Lancashire Lass:

I might be 63, but I am not dead. I like to look nice and feel comfortable at this age, but I'm not willing to settle for "old lady styles." I have been shopping at Tan Jay. They have come a long way over the years. I remember saying to my best friend, Lis, that I would NEVER shop at Tan Jay, and here we both are at Tan Jay and loving it. Once in a while I will go back to a designer shop if I want something really special, but I'm telling you it's hard to find something that both looks good and feels good and doesn't make me look like an old woman trying to look like a young one. Thanks again!

MirrorWoman:

The best "shopping" I have done in the last year was hiring a personal stylist who walked me through my closet, showed me what looked good on me, what doesn't—and why—and then put together some great outfits and a shopping list of additions I needed to complete my wardrobe. End result was I bought only a few things at Macy's and Nordstrom's (and The Rack) this year, and my clothes looked great. My fabulous stylist was honest about what made me look frumpy (rhinestones, loose-fitting styles) and were too young (Who made me buy those pink capris anyway???).

ON FINDING THE RIGHT JEANS
FROM A CONVERSATION ON VN

Whether it's the leading-edge Boomer and her memories of her first Levi's or trailing-edgers and their Calvin Kleins, jeans are part of the Vibrant Woman's legacy—and finding just the right pair remains central to her fashion mission.

FranS:

Hi, gosh, an opportunity to sound off about jeans. Two suggestions for jeans makers: If you're creating a pair of slacks for a lady with a large back, leave off the decorated back pockets. Better yet, leave off the back pockets altogether. I don't carry a wallet and I'm not trying to enlarge my butt, OK? I NEVER put stuff in any of my Levi pockets. Here's a HUGE leap: NO POCKETS! Next? Make a few pair without belt loops. Some ladies may always wear a belt with their jeans, but frankly, I never do so, and not many women do. Belt loops add a little more bulk where I don't need it. While I'm at it (I'm sorry, I can't stop), a blouse with attention drawn to the shoulder line? Very slimming. Short blouses with detail that draws the eye to the somewhat enlarged waistline of a lady my age (keep guessing)...those will stay on the rack in the store—where they should stay. I beg clothing designers to use some common sense and think "outside the box."

KarenT:

Your sound-off was worded perfectly!

BJM:

Right on, girl, you go!

Sewcrazy:

You go, girl. I've had it with all of them.

DebbieDeb:

I ordered a pair of denim "trouser" jeans (sz 12) from Talbots and JJill. Just received them, and they actually look/feel pretty nice. Cut so that my "muffin top" isn't bulging. No pockets on the tush, more of a relaxed bootcut, and a little more tailored, but cool looking. I'm 5'-8.5" so I like them long, and the JJill are 33" which is great for me. The Talbots are 32" which works for me when I wear flats. The final judgment of these jeans came from my 26-year-old daughter who stopped by this afternoon—I tried them on and she gave them a two thumbs-up! Definitely not "Mom" jeans. :)

ON AMBIVALENCE TOWARD AGING
FROM A CONVERSATION ON VN

"Hating that I'm starting to look old" vs "Realizing that true beauty is within and increases with age."

Crystalli:

I probably should have mulled this over longer, but here goes... bit by bit, I've gotten used to looking older, at least on some days. I'd been considered very attractive all my life and kind of relied on it to feel accepted. I did have plastic surgery in my 50s, a facelift, but now I definitely look like an older woman. I'm quite ambivalent about more procedures. If I had the money to splurge, I might. But, on the other hand, I'd like to be able to say to my pretty preteen granddaughter that there is a great deal more to her than her looks, that looks will fade but self-development will shine through as she becomes a poised, interesting, self-confident older woman. I would like to say this without feeling like a hypocrite. I would also like to fit in with women my own age, and be accepted for me, just as I am. Thinking of this fills me with a feeling of peace. No more poring over cosmetic surgery ads. Just to be not the one who is seen but the one who sees. I'm moving toward that place, and it's a good place to be. Thank you for asking the question. We each need to answer it for ourselves.

Suesan:

The problem isn't aging—it's not seeing the beauty in aging.

MagentaRose:

I also was very attractive...up until this year. It was like the Geritol commercial models: a few wrinkles and a quite becoming tuft of white hair. Then this year I've gained weight, my face has lost its firm contour, and my neck is wrinkly. There's some lines in "The Oldest Confederate Widow Tells All" that say something like: "It's really sad to see all those old women that were former beauties acting as if they're still pretty... they'd be well advised if somebody told them to think of something other than themselves," so:

I do what I can: 1) Dance every morning, 2) Went and got larger clothes that are nice (stopped waiting to lose weight), 3) Got some eyelash thing that's supposed to bring back my now almost nonexistent lashes—it does come with a warranty! and 4) Somebody in this site recommended Facial Magic exercises, and I'm going to try them. She said it helps to get rid of those vertical lip lines (I forgot to mention those).

Every morning I dance. This makes me feel really good, and with that feeling I move through the day. Nature's kind and makes us forget our pain and sorrows and lets us keep the image of our younger selves.

Don't try to look young. Try to look your best.

ON MENOPUDGE

BLOG BY ELLEN SARVER DOLGE, "MENOPUDGE KILLED MY WARDROBE"

The Vibrant Woman does her best to adapt to her changing body, with equal parts ofresourcefulness and humor.

It doesn't matter if you start out as a size 0 or a size 20; your body is going to change in menopause. I'm quite sure that one night as I was sleeping, the PM&M* alien came and put my body in a blender and turned it on high—nothing is where it used to be. I think that alien also shrank all my clothes.

I gravitated toward the looser clothes in my wardrobe, wearing the same things over and over. The rest of my clothes got dusty. I tried every diet, but I didn't lose a pound until I got my thyroid checked and hormones balanced. However, I have great news: in the interim, there are three magic answers to this problem:

1. The extra-large plastic garbage bag.

Go buy a box of the largest plastic garbage bags you can find. Fill up the bags with all those clothes that don't fit anymore and get rid of all that dust. My days were so much more joyful when I wasn't looking at those damn clothes every day. It was so liberating! The good news is that if you get your hormones balanced, you might be able to fit back into some of these things. So, save the bags in your storage closet or garage. In the meantime, I went out and bought a couple of pairs of pants that fit me. I didn't care what the hell size they were. I needed to feel comfortable. I threw in a few loose tops and dresses, and I was a new shmirshky!**

2. Spanx.

Spanx are sold everywhere. You wear them under your clothes to smooth out your figure. Think of them as a reverse balloon. Instead of blowing out and filling up, you're sucking in and smoothing down. They're incredible! At first, I thought that the smaller the Spanx, the better I would look. No! Do not buy Spanx so small that you break out in a sweat just struggling to pull them up. If you do, you will have a huge spillover at the waist. Plus, you will not be fun to be with if you can't breathe. In fact, you will be a bitch on wheels. Remember, you got rid of the clothes that cut off your circulation for a reason.

3. A seamstress.

If you have some special clothes that you can't get yourself to put in the large garbage bag or fit into with Spanx, get out your sewing kit or find a seamstress. Once, when I needed to go to a black-tie party, not one of my long gowns fit me, even with the "extra hold" Spanx. I sent out an SOS to a dear friend of mine for a recommendation of a good seamstress. I'd never met this seamstress before, but she immediately understood and fixed the dress for me. The Sisterhood to the rescue!

*PM&M: perimenopause and menopause
**shmirshky: vagina, woman

ON TAKING THE WALK OF FAME
BLOG BY MEIGLER, "BODACIOUS BOOMER"

The Vibrant Woman wants to look her best—but she wants comfort, too.

Evelyn sent me an e-mail this morning that just started my day off with a bang. Now I can't decide whether to feel bad about my T-Day indulges, get a cat o'nine tails and start flailing at my back like a possessed monk, or just become anorexic until the beginning of next year. And what was my wonderful friend nice enough to send me you ask?

She sent me an ad for Spanx!

Actually she sent it as a joke, knowing full well how I feel about them. I'm not advocating that everyone always has to go "au naturel" all the time. I think control top panty hose are great when you just need a little help to make you feel beautiful in a particular outfit. However, I don't think that putting on any foundation garment that takes three people to help you get into and EMS personnel with the "jaws of life" to get you out of can be a good thing. What if your true love has plied you with champagne and strawberries all night and you just can't wait? His Viagra has kicked in, and the clock is **ticking**. Do you really want to have to have him help you out of a garment that's holding on to you like a giant anaconda? There is just nothing sexy about that, unless you're into bondage; and from what I've seen, Spanx isn't nearly industrial enough for most of those folks.

ON DOES ANYBODY ELSE HAVE THIS PROBLEM?
FROM A CONVERSATION ON VN

Vibrant Women turn to one another both to offer support and to find solutions that aren't otherwise being addressed.

RobinSue:

Does anyone else have a problem with facial hair? I have a lot of hair on my chin that I find myself setting and plucking every night.

Just Leav...:

OMG hair management has become quite time consuming. Every time I think I've got it all under control, it's time to start all over. I have started using something you may have seen on TV called a Tweezy. It pretty much plucks your facial hair at lightening speed. Yes, it hurts. Mostly at first and then it either numbs you or you just get used to it. I only do my lip and chin areas. Then I use the trimmer you see on TV to keep my eyebrows under control, and sometimes for my nose hair, although it's not designed for that. All of that is just for my face! Not to mention the rest of me!! I have to do this about every three days or no longer than a week. Grr. If you have any tips on streamlining hair management...please let me know.

Angel:

I too have a Tweezy. It hurts a little, but it sure beats plucking or shaving! I also have a nose hair trimmer! GRRRRR Whoever said this stage of life was great....didn't know what they were talking about. I have to shave, pluck, or tweeze places that I never had hair before. So much for getting older.........;-)))

lauriebh:

It's a natural response to shifting hormones, and it's hereditary. There are lots of choices—waxes, bleach, mini shavers, or a combination of all three. Set up a buddy system with a friend to remind you to go on stray hair patrol before a special occasion, and cheer up! You're still a woman!!!!

ON FEELING FAT

BLOG BY SARAH GAYLE CARTER

The Vibrant Woman often cares about her weight, but after a lifetime of dieting, still doesn't always have a handle on it.

I arrived in Arizona on New Year's Day, slightly disoriented, but game. After last year's first foray into the brave new world of acres of desert, cactus, and retirees, at least I was prepared. So here I am, back again. Back to these great, desert expanses of bare earth, broad sky, and raw, relentless sunshine. Leaving behind three weeks of Chistmas-ing in Richmond with family and friends, our wonderful barn in Maine nestled cozily amid the snow and ice of New England winter, and a full year of slow but steady, then fast and furious weight gain.

I'm fat again. Really fat.

I know what you're thinking, "Well honey, what did you expect? You with the eggnog, cookie dough, candy, butter-cream cheese-crab concoction? You with the 'what would Christmas be without food and the pre-pre-ordained holiday license to dispense with calorie awareness and indulge with abandon?'"

Well, I'm here to tell you, the chickens (and the calories!) have come home to roost, and it's NOT a pretty picture.

But, in all fairness, this is not really about a three-week Christmas food fest—whipping cream, eggnog, and all. That alone would amount to no more than a mildly serious but temporary stumble from grace, or consciousness more like it. This is about a complicated and, for me, long running struggle to come to grips with my habit of "feeding" myself inappropriately. Going numb around food. I haven't felt that out of control for a very long time. I thought I was through with crash and burn, totally self-defeating, almost self-punishing, behavior. Guess not. Old triggers being what they are powerful programming, it didn't take much to slip across the invisible and oh-so-subtle line into self-destruction. Here's the thing: I've done a lot of work on this issue, years and years of it. For something like twenty-five years, I've been learning about how to eat healthily. It was a gradual shift, but for a long time now, I've rarely eaten fast food, fake food, bags of chips, diet drinks, caffeine, or soft drinks of any kind. I'm an herbal tea, yogurt, granola, organic as often as possible kind of girl. I long ago woke up to the "dead end" of the diet syndrome, having spent years bouncing from Atkins to Ornish to grapefruit, and everything in between. And, looking back on it, I wasn't even fat! I've seen old photos of myself in my 20s when all this started, I look great. What I wouldn't give for that figure again. But I remember myself then, worrying that I was fat, buying the original Atkins Diet book, the first of many "diets" to come. I'm a textbook case—a young female made to feel fat, who jumped into a series of diets that seem to have created the very problem I was afraid of, i.e. being "fat." Not to mention this whole love/hate thing around food. The more tightly I held the reins, the wilder the horse became.

Slowly, patiently, oh so gradually, I thought I had tamed the wild horse. I gave him his head. I allowed my mind and my body to trust again that food was not the enemy, that my body was not the enemy. I stopped hating myself and fearing food. Fearing myself and hating the hold food had on me. I ate what I wanted when I was hungry, sticking to "real" foods I knew were better choices—whole grains, unrefined sugars, enough protein, but all in much smaller quantities. You'd be surprised how little it really takes to keep you satisfied till the next meal. And if I was hungry, I ate something. No big deal. I loosened the grip of absolutes. I didn't stress myself or worry if "the plan" fell apart from time to time and I ate more than I needed, or had sugar, or whatever. This was life, not a diet. I just picked up the thread again—no guilt, no blame. And I knew I had to move, to use my body. I committed—again—to exercise. For me it's walking. Just short of four miles a day took me about 50 minutes every morning. Over the course of a year, with great ease, I lost 30 plus pounds.

Now it's back—and more.

It was my "wanting" mind, that beaten down, punished, wayward, wanton, angry child who staged the temper tantrums that brought me back to overindulging (punishing myself?) with food. It started innocently enough, moving to Maine, time on my hands, loving to cook, and with Russ as an appreciative audience, I began to eat more than I really needed and exercised less, then almost not at all. Occasional treats became regular fixtures—wine with dinner, dessert, cookies with my afternoon tea. At some point, the balance tipped, both chemical and psychological. There I was, lost again. And feeling bad about it only made me dive in deeper—how weird is that? By the time I arrived in Richmond, I had decided to initiate crash-and-burn mode. To blow it out, to push myself off the deep end. It worked. By the last few days there, I couldn't even make myself eat the leftover ginger cookies. I let the doughnuts go stale. I threw away the rest of the eggnog.

I was thoroughly disgusted with myself. It didn't feel good. And worse so now having such a vivid and recent memory of life without the compulsive push and pull of food. So here I am in the desert. A minimalist setting if there ever was one. (Have I mentioned the tortured plant life making do on next to nothing?) A great place for a dose of spartan self-restraint, don't you think? I've only been here a few days, but so far, I'm having no problem happily taking up that tool of all tools: discipline. Fake it till you make it. The sugar will wash out of my system soon enough, the warm air will clear my muddled, wanting mind, and my muscles will respond eagerly to my call to action (surely they're still in there somewhere under this layer of alien flesh). I've done it before; I'll do it again. I'm giving myself this entire new year to lose 45 pounds. Yes, shocking but true, I've gained that much more than I'd lost before.

Welcome 2010. A new year, a new beginning.

ON LIKING MYSELF
FROM A CONVERSATION ON VN

"We have more to offer than our fading looks and our attempts to cover it up. We have our inner beauty that spills over in our smiles and our kindness and our no nonsense approach."

SatorisWings:

If you want to wear makeup, wear it. But most women, as the visual acuity diminishes, put on makeup in such a way that it looks awful. The mascara gets on the sagging eyelid folds, the blush is too thick. I remember old ladies doing it when I was young. Now I see my generation doing it too. To me, the makeup just says that we don't accept ourselves the way we are. My lips still have a lot of natural color. The rest of it—who cares. I must admit I do look in the mirror at times and think, look at that. Yuck. But the bottom line is that I like myself. I like who I am and what I've become. No matter what I do I will not look like I looked at 20, 35, or 49. I exercise fifty minutes a day to keep things working and to avoid medication. So the body doesn't look bad for my age. But that's the key—for my age. The hair is getting streaked with white and turning wavy. I actually like the white and the waves. I cheer it on. I've had terminally straight hair. What I dislike the most is that the fatigue and sadness are more noticeable on my face when I'm tired, stressed, and sad. What I go for is sparkle, and that comes from within. That means I work on overcoming all the horrid things that happen to me, and I am happy in spite of them and stronger because of them. I'm 60. I had a major pout about turning 50. But by 60, it was just an interesting event, me being 60. I hope I can look at 70 and 80 the same way, if not better.

We are the next generation of crones—in our infancy. The world is a mess and needs us, needs our hard-earned wisdom, even if it doesn't acknowledge it. That's why I'm writing old lady stories now. As Madeline Albright said of the mess in the Middle East, "A bunch of old grandmothers could have it cleared up in a year and a half." We have more to offer than our fading looks and our attempts to cover it up. We have our inner beauty that spills over in our smiles and our kindness and our no nonsense approach.

[1]"Fashion Survey" (survey, VibrantNation.com, March 3, 2010), http://www.vibrantnation.com/assets/2805/Vibrant_Nation_fashion_release_final.pdf.

[2]Ibid.

[3]Ibid.

5

THE REINVENTION OF WORK:

Seeking Purpose in the New Gig Economy

The Vibrant Woman at work is resourceful, opportunistic, and creative —because it's in her nature, and because she has no choice. Even those who are relying on unemployment or early Social Security to make ends meet are somehow managing to remain confident about the possibilities.

The Vibrant Woman is navigating her 50s and 60s believing that as much as she's already accomplished, there's much more to do. Some of her passion for work has been driven by need. In the aftermath of the great recession, she realizes that she's behind in her plans to make money and to set aside funds for later in life. But even when money is not an issue, she still wants to make full use of her abilities and to be recognized for her contributions.

This drive to make things happen is nothing new for her. The Vibrant Woman came of age as part of the largest, most educated generation of women in history. She quickly discovered that she had to stand out to get noticed. And so she was often the girl in the classroom, hand up in the air, who knew all the answers. She took that same competitive spirit to work with her, adding accomplishments outside the house on top of her traditional aspirations to be a good mom, friend, and wife. She has also sought to be physically fit, look great, and entertain beautifully. Of course, her achievements often came at the expense of her learning how to self-nurture or relax. In fact, she is the first generation for whom achieving status as a "Superwoman" was implanted in her DNA. It's not that Vibrant Women don't go on retreats, take yoga, or learn to meditate. But even when they do, they find themselves working just as hard in search of the ever-elusive goal of work-life balance.

A WORKPLACE REVOLUTION

Coupled with her efforts to stand out from the crowd, the Vibrant Woman who came of age in the era of women's liberation is all too aware of how hard she had to work to collect on the promise of gender equality. Regardless of the difficulties she encountered forging new ground for women in organizational life, she managed to remain energized by the sense that what she was doing was part of something greater than herself. By doing so, she created a workplace revolution. And while her daughters generally take it for granted that they may enter and progress in the fields of their choice, she knows exactly what she has accomplished not only for herself but for all the generations of women to come.

It is both poignant and ironic that now, just when the Vibrant Woman expected to be at the peak of her career, she's finding herself once again having to invest valuable energy negotiating a new relationship to the status quo. In fact, nobody is more surprised than the Vibrant Woman to be at this age and stage in life, only to discover that the institutions she has served so well and long have found her lifetime of workplace experience largely expendable.

Should the 50+ woman lie about her age on her résumé?

There are many, even among the elite of 50+ female CEOs, nonprofit directors, heads of human resources, physicians, realtors, educators, and publishing and marketing industry executives who are facing the reality of the post-recession work environment: downsizing. But it isn't just the recession that is moving women 50+ out of the corner office. While she wasn't the first to be shown the way (the men of her generation had that dubious distinction), she has discovered that behind the insidious mask of the sexism she has bucked throughout her career is yet another "ism": ageism.

One of the first explosive conversations on VibrantNation.com asked a simple question. Should the 50+ woman lie about her age on her résumé? The underlying premise that the length and depth of her experience have become a liability is not even questioned as women consider the pros and cons of listing dates next to their degrees. Having broken or at least cracked the glass ceiling, she now stands accused by younger generations for having become a ceiling of her own: this one "gray."[1]

THE GRAY CEILING

"The gray ceiling" is a metaphor describing the positions at the top of organizational life still occupied by Boomer men and women and the attendant frustration that younger generations feel as they review their prospects for career advancement. At an age when generations past would have graciously passed off the reins, Boomers have neither the savings nor the diminishment of the appetite for work that once gave "retirement" its appeal. Meanwhile, the skills they have gained at work are more relevant than ever. A study of 50+ workers by the management consultant firm Towers Perrin for AARP found that "talented experienced workers have distinct performance advantages in roles that require advanced skills, training, experience, and knowledge of a company's business processes, people, or customers."[2]

Mentally sharp and benefiting from a lifetime of experience, Boomers remain theoretically capable of remaining at work for the next fifteen years; this presents a challenge business has never before had to face. In fact, our era represents the first time in history that four generations are at work simultaneously, each vying for recognition, compensation, and power. The Ikes, those born between 1932 and 1945, are finishing up the work of "The Greatest Generation." Generations X (1965-1979) and Y (1980 and beyond) are claiming their places and carving out their niches. And increasingly, those niches are coming at the expense of the crowning glory of compensation, power, and respect for which Boomer women have paid plenty of dues.

The younger generations are increasingly impatient waiting their turn. And whenever there is an advantage to be seized, many of them—including the Vibrant Woman's own sons and daughters—are more than ready to take full advantage.

ONE REVOLUTION TOO MANY

Fighting the battle of ageism in the workplace—particularly when tinged by the residues of sexism that continue to hold sway in many organizations and industries—may be one revolution too many, even for the most vibrant of woman. While some women are in denial, believing that seniority will provide some degree of protection from age discrimination, the majority feel that they have been betrayed by the generational politics of the traditional workplace. Others, feeling the residues of guilt about having turned her own offspring into latchkey kids, believe that it is their duty to step aside to make room for the next generation of leadership. Whatever the reason, many Vibrant Women are now actively seeking and pursuing alternatives that will help them regain control over their lives. And they are increasingly willing to dig deep into their own resources—intellectual, spiritual, and financial—to fund the transition to what's next.

SEEKING THE WORK SHE WANTS

When the Vibrant Woman ponders "what's next," old notions of retirement are not even a consideration. Traditionally, retirement meant the end of work, accompanied by fantasies of never-ending rounds of golf or strolls down exotic, sandy beaches. But in a landmark study, MetLife reported that 75 percent of workers continue to plan to work in some capacity past retirement age.[3]

When referring to her generation, the Vibrant Woman uses the word "retirement" only in the context of the phrase "work after retirement," telling us that "retirement" has changed its meaning, to the degree it has retained any meaning whatsoever. In fact, when Vibrant Women use "retirement" as a stand-alone word, she is either

MetLife reported that 75 percent of workers continue to plan to work in some capacity past retirement age.

referring to her parents' generation or talking about some abstract future time when she will be "too old or sick to work." This woman is not withdrawing or retreating. Rather she's looking forward, believing that her best work years are still ahead of her.

Turning her back on traditional notions of retirement, she prefers to think of this promising "what's next" as "reinvention." The concept of reinvention has inspired thousands of books with "reinvention" in the title. More magazine produces an annual Reinvention Convention, and legions of life coaches, many of them former denizens of the corporate community, have hung up their shingles, ready to midwife "the reinvention process" at rates of $200 or more an hour.

While the word "reinvention" suggests control, the reality is more about adaptation through trial and error, an often somewhat messier affair. For example, one member of the Vibrant Nation community decided to reinvent her life by using the proceeds from selling the Los Angeles restaurant she'd spent her career building to fund a business importing crafts from Spain. Of course, she'd be moving to Spain. We were surprised to hear that a year after a grand send-off, she was back in Los Angeles. Our member, as it turned out, was one of the millionaires (and not the only VibrantNation.com member) who lost it all in the Madoff ponzi scheme. When she was asked if she was still going to be able to fund her start-up import business, she replied: "No. Lost it all. Now I'm looking for a job in the hotel catering business in L.A. Do you know of anything?"

"But what about your dream of living in Spain?"

"I was ready to come home anyway. You know me. What's next?"

Last we heard, she was being trailed by cameras, auditioning for a reality show that would chronicle her efforts to land a job.

Our member's vibrant spirit is admirable and epitomizes a kind of pioneer spunkiness, ready to conquer whatever challenges life throws at her as if the issues had actually been self-selected.

ENCORE CAREERS—OR RECOVERY?

While Vibrant Women admire this degree of verve, many do not go through their own reinvention transitions so cheerfully. In fact, many present an upbeat exterior to the world while secretly kicking and screaming their way toward their "encore career"—a term that itself implies a victory lap rather than the forced restart it feels like, at least while in the throes of the early stages of transition.[4] Such women are often unhappily surprised to find themselves ricocheting between levels of panic and self-blame that they had hoped to have left behind. Even when their despair proves to be transitional, it feels deeply painful and undeserved.[5]

In its wake, more than a few find themselves back on the road to recovery by drawing down retirement savings to fund start-ups and taking education loans to go back to school for training in new fields. Vibrant Women struggle with their insecurities, as they are forced

"No one I know has a job anymore,"

to balance their urge to preserve and protect whatever savings they've been able to accumulate against the prospect of investing in themselves. More often than not, judicious risks on their own behalf prevail. Not long ago, one member of VibrantNation.com asked the community: "Should I use rainy day funds to fund my transition?" To which another member replied: "What do you think the rainy day funds are for?"

THE GIG ECONOMY

In the early stages of the recession, Tina Brown declared that we are in "the gig economy": "No one I know has a job anymore," she wrote. "They've got gigs…a bunch of free-floating projects, consultancies, and part-time bits and pieces they try and stitch together to make what they refer to wryly as 'the Nut.'"[6]

For Vibrant Women, living in a gig economy means that in addition to starting their own companies and going back to school—both of which are taking place to an unprecedented degree—they are piecing together alternative livelihoods as skillfully as women of previous generations assembled patchwork quilts. In this case, the material being fashioned into a whole consists of the odd assortment of hobbies, skills, opportunities, and income-generating compromises.

While we don't hear Vibrant Women talk in terms of "making their nut," they are succeeding at patching together new and often improved work situations for themselves. Many are trying to find the right mix of consulting gigs to replace the full-time job they have lost. Others are patching in ways to make a contribution or create meaning that full-time work doesn't allow. Some who put their careers on hold or felt torn between work and family through the course of their work lives are newly energized by having finally achieved an age and stage in life where they can pursue their ambitions without ambivalence. Finally, there are those who still need the flexibility from part-time work to accommodate the needs of family members who still or newly need their help: aging parents or adult children who have returned home, sometimes with grandchildren in tow. The gig economy is an advantage for these women because it allows them, at least in theory, the freedom to control their own job description and to satisfy their varied needs and interests.

But working the gig economy has disadvantages, as well. Few Vibrant Women are making the same kind of money, to say nothing of benefits, from gigs that a "real" job provides. She is working harder than ever, maintaining her social and business networks not only for personal gratification but to self-create as many opportunities as possible. Sometimes her new gig can become a business of its own, and the irrepressible Vibrant Woman is once again perfectly positioned to micro-target the consumer she

---

Many are trying to find the right mix of consulting gigs to replace the full-time job they have lost.

---

knows best. Women over 50 are four times more likely to be self-employed than working for others, starting more businesses than any other demographic. Many focus on the needs of other women like themselves, including entrepreneurs like Tomima Edmark, who used her understanding of women's shopping frustrations and needs to create www.herroom.com, the user-friendly, review-based website we referenced in chapter 4, that sells lingerie and bras. Cell phone pioneer Arlene Harris created the simple-to-use Jitterbug phone because she knew how hard it was to get older parents wired. Others, like Georgina Callan, whose Curtain Exchange retail business is mostly franchised by other women 50+ like her, build businesses that piggyback on the entrepreneurial energy of other Vibrant Woman.

THE NEW VOLUNTEER

For the Vibrant Woman who cannot find a paying gig, doesn't need it, or who has time to give back, volunteering is an important form of work. In keeping with her attitude about contributing at the highest level of her ability, it is not enough for the Vibrant Woman to report for duty to various volunteer opportunities, charities, and nonprofits, availing themselves of just any opportunity to "make myself useful." Whereas her mother's generation may have been content to stuff envelopes and serve up soup, the Vibrant Woman

Women over 50 are four times more likely to be self-employed than working for others,

wants to be utilized to the peak of her ability. Even when unpaid, she is not averse to taking on real responsibility. In fact, offer her any less, and she may well go out and start a competitive nonprofit of her own. However thrown together her career may look from the outside in, do not make the mistake of believing that she's "dabbling" with her work. Even those who are independently wealthy want, above all, to be taken seriously.

The Vibrant Woman at work is resourceful, opportunistic, and creative—because it's in her nature and because she has no choice. Even those who are relying on unemployment or early Social Security to make ends meet are somehow managing to remain confident about the possibilities. While we hope this approach will find its right reward, it also gives many demographic experts pause to consider not whether but how deeply this woman is in denial about what the future may hold for her.

As we will see in chapter 6, when she thinks about such practical concerns as long-term financial security, health insurance, and the like, her confidence in institutional support has suffered major blows. But about her ability to find meaning through work, the Vibrant Woman remains excited about what lies ahead.

IMPLICATIONS FOR MARKETERS

The Vibrant Woman may have teenaged or adult children at home—or not. She may be married—or not. She may have grandchildren—or not. But the one thing marketers can know about her for sure: she is serious about her work. The irony is that despite this fact, so many marketers persist in showing images of her in the kitchen, at yoga class, at the park, and doing everything but work.

Here are some key points for marketers to keep in mind:

> Don't forget the purchasing power of self-employed women. That means they spend more money in all kinds of business-oriented categories, from hardware to software, office supplies, financial services, and healthcare. Show her images she can identify with of women her age staying at business hotels, using technology to stay connected, and so on. Not only will these ads catch her eyes but her business, as well.

> Recognize that she is working and wants to find meaning through work as long as she can. If you are marketing a pharmaceutical brand to Boomer women, for instance, do so in the context of her working life. A recent ad for Depends gets it right. The ad centers on the engaging image of a woman conducting an orchestra. The ad succeeds in demonstrating how use of their product can make it easier for their customer to work in spite of a physical condition, without reducing her to an invalid. Even when a woman has an issue that limits her in some way, assume that she still wants to—and can—make a difference.

> **Don't use the word "retirement."** As we said earlier, when the Vibrant Woman hears that term, she will think you are either referring to her parents or talking about some time in the distant future when she will be too old or sick to work. If you provide financial services, talk about the Vibrant Woman's "financial future." If you want to connect with her aspirations, speak in terms of giving her the increased freedom to pick and choose how and where she will contribute through the full utilization of her skills and abilities. Listen to women like VibrantNation.com member realestatelady, who said "Ten years ago I was more ready to retire than currently." Or another, Donna, who said, "Now that I work for myself…I don't think I'll ever retire."

> **Believe in her.** In spite of setbacks, layoffs, ageism, and all the career-related challenges the Vibrant Woman has faced, she remains optimistic in her search for meaning through work. She may complain about the professional challenges she faces, but if you complain on her behalf she will think you're talking down to her. Believe in her and take her aspirations seriously, no matter how large the gap you see between her current circumstances and her perception of herself.

> **Use her to market for you.** Most self-employed Vibrant Women embrace their roles as promoters. This entrepreneurial-minded woman is highly networked and relishes her role as influencer. Because the most important referral source for Vibrant Women is other women like them, smart marketers will use those who are working directly with their peers as consultants, coaches, realtors, bloggers, teachers, travel agents, and so on to deliver their message.

> **Engage her inner philanthropist.** Avoid superficial "cause marketing" approaches that she will read as cynical ploys to get her to spend money on a particular brand. Rather, recognize that for many Vibrant Women, their work is inseparable from their desire to make the world a better place. Demonstrate how your work, like theirs, combines a profit motive with the genuine desire to give back.

> **Recruit her.** The Vibrant Woman wants to work. She has great experience. And she intimately understands the fast-growing market you should be paying more attention to: Vibrant Women like her.

The Voices of Vibrant Nation

Ageism is a workplace reality for Vibrant Women, and many have preferred to leave toxic environments rather than fight one more battle. However, those who are hanging in bring a level of resourcefulness—and more than a touch of humor—to the challenges of the four-generation workplace.

EIGHT WAYS NOT TO ACT OLD AT WORK
FROM A CONVERSATION ON VN*

One of the upsides for some of growing older in the work environment is getting to spend less time worrying about fitting in with younger colleagues.

Nettie:

I don't consider myself as "old".....What is age really....only numbers!

I went back to earn a college degree at 61 and because of that got a top-notch job in another dept. when mine was phased out. Was retired in 2007 and decided I needed to work. ....Now at a very young 72 I am working part-time every day and loving it. My younger coworkers treat me as an equal..... no one talks about age. Yes, I get my hair styled once a month and my nails receive a "French" manicure regularly.

Remember that "AGE" is only a word. What really matters is how one feels; how one can live one's life well and get along with others of varying ages. We are all in this together. It is all about Attitude.

Jean T:

I think there is a difference between "old" and "mature." Many young people are quite mature, and many people with many years are "old" rather than mature. I do not have to listen to the most bizarre music to "not be old," but I can avoid making comments that show how old I am. As in "When I was your age."

Sophie:

You know I hate to be cynical, but it doesn't really matter what I do or how I do it, I find that once you're a certain age and a woman, you're fairly invisible. I find that younger colleagues and male colleagues my own age and older routinely tune me out and treat me as though I'm not there. So, the upside is I don't have to spend a lot of time fitting in with the younger crowd because when you're invisible, you can do what you please, how you please, as long as the work gets done.

Lynnette:

GOOD ONE! I was offended and hurt at first that this was happening to me. Glad to hear it is not just me, but you are right, if they chose to tune you out...do what you want!!!!

*From a conversation based on Pamela Redmond Satran's book *How Not to Act Old* (New York: HarperCollins Publishers, 2009)

WHAT'S IT REALLY LIKE TO RETURN TO SCHOOL AFTER 50?
BLOG BY SEAWRITER, "ONE HEART, MANY GARDENS"

Many Vibrant Women are considering returning to school to be trained in new fields, advance their old careers, or simply pursue personal enrichment. But she doesn't make the decision lightly.

I feared being the older woman in the back of the classroom, the person whose very presence caused the younger students to lower their voices and watch their language—the one who never said anything but took constant and copious notes.

I thought I would be older than the professors. I thought I would feel as if I were in class with my daughters and their friends, trying to crash through the age-cohort barriers with the same success as middle-aged women wearing headbands and hiphuggers met when I was an undergraduate in the 1970s. Don't they have anything more appropriate to do with their time? Like go somewhere else and be old?

Let's put first things first: because I have daughters of my own, I have years of practice discerning which styles and articles of clothing can cross over into my closet and which absolutely cannot. I'd like to think I'd know better even without the training grounds my daughters provided, though I'll never know. At least I'm confident I am not at risk for dressing inappropriately.

Secondly, though I've been away from the classroom for many years, I haven't rented out the space between my ears. I've read many times more books since getting my BA than I did up until then, and I have experienced exponential growth in the number of topics that interest me. Everything I learn builds upon everything that came before; I sense that the roots of wisdom have been laid down.

My papers are coherent, and writing them fascinates me. It is a pleasure to grapple with a narrow topic and discuss it logically within a limited framework of seven or ten pages. Assignments become like excursions into areas I'd probably be reading about anyway, only this time the instructor serves as a professional guide for the expedition. Questions can be asked and discussed; Google is no longer my main portal for information.

The other advantage I bring to my studies is the scope of experience that only derives from meeting the changing demands of life year after year. Confidence and preparedness for whatever may come next are earmarks of the returning student. Coursework often falls into already established categories. I already know a little about a lot of what we cover in class. Encountering new topics and refining the old becomes an immensely satisfying process.

As for stamina—it is amazing how energizing it is to undertake a project that fascinates and makes demands of you. Yes, most of the students are younger than I am, but there is also a rather large group of individuals who are returning to school to redirect their careers, to learn skills for re-entering the job force, or to reimmerse themselves in the world of academia after a long absence of child-rearing or career building—or both. As it turns out, I'm not even the oldest person in my program, the professors are older than I am, and I certainly wouldn't call myself the quiet older woman in the back of the classroom.

DO WOMEN MAKE BETTER ENTREPRENEURS?
FROM A CONVERSATION ON VN

Vibrant Women not only believe they have what it takes to start their own companies, but they believe they have a competitive advantage.

Michelle M.:

As one woman in the ripe and right time to be an entrepreneur, what shapes my entrepreneurial style most is the power of connecting. Making, sustaining, and celebrating connection is the thread that runs through my entrepreneurial fiber. I do it without thinking. While men have the "good ol' boys" way of networking, often played out on the golf course or on a racquetball court, it's more than that for many women, me included. I think women connect at a deeper level as part of an ongoing conversation.

I know being a woman has shaped me for sure in one other way as an entrepreneur! Having spent enough time in cars with men, one big difference is that I'm comfortable saying "I don't know, let's stop the car and ask." I'll actively seek out someone who can give me guidance when I'm lost and can't see the forest for the trees: I don't see it as a dent in my ego.

I think being a woman has an impact on how I listen, too. I absorb everything: the words spoken, the tone, the facial expression, the body language. When I worked in a corporate office, it's what made me get up out of my chair and go talk to someone instead of dashing off an e-mail or picking up the phone. I wanted a whole picture. Entrepreneurially, that's how I operate, too, whenever I can.

My being a woman also shapes how I collaborate. When I pull people in to a project or task, I look for ways to enhance that experience for them so that when it's completed, they walk away having received as much or more than I do. And they can't wait to collaborate again!

ON REINVENTING HERSELF
FROM A CONVERSATION ON VN

"Some years back, when I was in the training and development field we would quote some number of times—think it was 5—that one would change one's career path in a lifetime. That has certainly been true for many, myself included. I would imagine that that career path change may have increased and will continue to do so as we go forward."

Triska:

Are other women my age reinventing themselves? In 2007, at the ripe young age of 56, I reinvented myself—learned digital photography and web development. I launched a business two months ago in pet and wildlife photography. Due to the economy and its current limitations, I've no business yet but great products! I am determined to keep marketing and publishing my blog. I'd love to network with other women my age who find themselves in a similar situation.

aid:

I am 60 and facing the "new retirement." Retirement as we all dream about living a life of leisure and pleasure is not the same anymore. When our folks retired, they weren't expected to live very long, so they only had to figure maybe five or ten years. But at 60 with my genetic history and providing the Beer Truck doesn't hit me, I can expect to live well into my 90s if not past 100. That gives me about thirty years after I reach full retirement age, which for me is 66. I think turning 60 became a sort of life crisis because I realized the full extent of what retirement actually meant in the twenty-first century. As a result, I think it becomes necessary for women to reinvent themselves by doing the things that they would do if they didn't have to worry about getting paid. For me it's writing. Most of my life I've had the seeds of novels dancing in my head. Now I have started writing them down, and who knows I might become a best-seller. What I will have done is written as if I didn't have to earn money. To write with passion is my goal. That and being warmer.

Triska:

My hat is off to you! If you're doing what you are passionate about, then it doesn't seem like "work." I used to say that I could never afford to retire with all the things I want to do (e.g., travel) and get (e.g., lenses for my photography). Now I think I would never WANT to retire. Sometimes, I feel guilty because I'm having so much fun, even doing grunt work. Good luck with your novels, and as for being warmer, you could always move to Florida.

ON INVALIDATION
FROM A CONVERSATION ON VN

Even when they are supposedly at the peak of their careers, many Vibrant Women still struggle against both ageism and sexism.

Dynamomma:

Have you ever thought about invalidation in more ways than the emotional verbal ways? All our lives we have heard comments from others like "Oh you don't really feel that way." Or, "Buck up and get over it." We see it a lot in relationships of parent/child, teacher/student, leader/follower, boss/employee, spouse A/spouse B. We've all experienced it and probably done it. But I'm talking about the invalidation of not being honored for the knowledge and experience you have gained from years of education and career involvement. If you are a professional in some field, there should be a level of honor given to what you "know." I'm not talking about an opinion. There's plenty of opinions. I'm talking about irrefutable facts that dictate outcomes and people's behaviors. I said to my husband the other day, "You are an electrician. You are a professional. If I had an electrical problem and you told me to put my finger in the electrical socket and hold it for three seconds because that would fix my problem, I would do it." Do you know what I'm talking about? This is a silly analogy, but it explains the honor I have for his expertise in this area. Do you ever feel that you are not validated for what you have developed over the years into an expertise? An expertise that is used for the betterment of all concerned in your life. I'm sure there are other words that describe this same feeling. But the word just hit me like a freight train. I've been feeling invalidated. It makes me feel sick to my stomach. Talk to me about this, OK?

jforth:

I am experiencing this as we speak! I am the CEO of a real estate industry trade association. I have been doing this for twenty-five years. Recently I came back from an industry conference and was very excited about a new web communications platform that would fit beautifully into our new strategic plan. I presented it to my board of directors, and they looked at me like I had two heads! I learned that you are never an expert in your own backyard. Long story short, they formed a task force to look at this program, and I am confident that they will go with it. However, I am very hurt and astonished that they wouldn't even look at it when I brought it up to them! I wasn't asking them to commit to it; just to look at it! As I have blogged about before, at 62, I am becoming invisible and do not get the respect my years and dedication should afford. Now that I've said it, I guess that's the cycle of life; when I was in my 20s and 30s I guess I would have thought how can this old broad know about technology? She should just retire! I am sure they said that behind my back. What a life lesson, even at my age!

Moongoddess:

It's frustrating. Having your expertise being "pooh-poohed" and then watching the wheel being reinvented makes it twofold.

Watermusic:

It's a little like being Michael Jordan on a losing basketball team and the coach won't put me in the game.

ON CREATING PURPOSE
VN INTERVIEW WITH VIBRANT GIVER KARON WRIGHT

Vibrant Women will go to great lengths to know that they are using their skills to make a difference. If they can't find an existing volunteer opportunity that will satisfy this need, they will fund their own start-up nonprofit.

In her corporate life, Karon Wright leads Achievement Partners, Inc., a performance management consulting, training, and coaching firm dedicated to creating stronger, more collaborative, and more productive working relationships for teams and individuals. But she is also Executive Director of The Greater Contribution, a not-for-profit organization dedicated to poverty relief worldwide.

Driven by a desire to give back to the world in the most significant way possible, Karon Wright founded The Greater Contribution with three colleagues in order to help people suffering from hunger, poverty, disease, natural disasters, and war. The nonprofit agency does this by raising awareness and funds to support developmental efforts and emergency relief around the world.

Funds raised by The Greater Contribution become micro-loans, which are loaned out and repaid over and over again. These small loans transform lives—giving families a way out of poverty with a sustainable income, regular food, shelter, health care, and education.

1. When and how did you begin to devote yourself more to giving back?

For seven years I've been attending an executive women's breakfast retreat where we focused on issues of women in the workplace. Then, about three years ago, I realized that I wanted to do more than teach executives to work more effectively. I wanted to do something more urgent in the grand scheme of things. I shared this with the other women at the breakfast retreat, and three women said, "We're with you. What will we do?"

2. What do you love most about the cause you support?

I'm a former teacher and a great believer in the power and importance of education. That's the really fun part of our work in The Greater Contribution. We talk about the huge need or the power of micro-loans, and at first people have no idea. But then they get very excited. They get it. The Greater Contribution is structured as a venue for people who want to help, so they can participate and give back. We offer several different programs for people to get involved. It's wonderful when someone gets what we're doing, and then decides they want to volunteer their own time to help.

What I love most, though, is seeing how what we're doing has made a difference in someone's life. Several times a year we receive reports about how our work is impacting specific women in developing areas around the world. We just got a report back from Malawi about the first village bank we sponsored. There's a photo of ten women with little babies on their laps and information about how the women are using the micro-loans we made possible to turn their lives around by creating sustainable income. They've started all kinds of businesses with these micro-loans—everything from goat meat to fish to secondhand clothing to cooking oil. These women and their families will not just have a few extra meals. Because of the work we do, these women will be sending their kids to school and breaking the cycle of poverty. The success stories are my reward. They're what really touch my heart.

At The Greater Contribution, I work with the most amazing women. They keep coming out of the woodwork because they want to give too. They have such an energy around doing this, and they have the kindest hearts you can imagine. It's heartwarming to see that people care so much about other people halfway around the world whom they will probably never see face to face. For us, it's about equal opportunity. The women we help happen to have been born in Malawi rather than Thousand Oaks, California. All they want is the same opportunity that women in the United States have all the time—to make a living from their hard work and the things that they make.

ON REINVENTING FREEDOM
BLOG BY CAROL ORSBORN, "INSIDE THE NATION"

The Vibrant Woman wants the right to work as long as she can, but she assumed that at the peak of her career, she would have the freedom to pick and choose her opportunities. With the recession, she's finding herself in a position where she is having to reinvent not only her livelihood but her definition of freedom.

Demographic researchers have floated survey after survey over the years, finding that even when Boomers anticipated having more than enough resources to retire, eight out of ten of us expected that we would continue working indefinitely.

Back then, a long couple of years ago, the right to work as long as we wanted to was a life-affirming rallying cry, reminiscent of all the previous revolutionary moves our generation has made over the years. Our generation-wide postponement of even revised notions of retirement was, in fact, the archetypal expression of our lifelong devotion to the quality we value most. Not status. Not even comfort. Rather, it is freedom: the ability to choose our own destinies.

We insisted that the men of our generation be able to grow their hair as long as they wanted. And the women bust through the glass ceiling to new heights in their careers. And then, when the surveyors called, we answered in unison: Nobody was going to tell us when, whether, or how to retire. We would work as long as we wanted to, and that was going to be for a long, long time.

For Boomers, freedom has always been among the highest of our generational ideals. So here's the irony. Because of the recession, we've proved the surveyors right. Postponing retirement "indefinitely" has become for many of us a reality. Not only for the reasons we thought, however, but also because we need the money. Those of us who are fortunate may have kept our jobs or found new ways to make money. But most of us share something in common. We have lost the freedom to make the choice of whether to work or not. Despite this loss, our generation continues to hold tight to our determination to have freedom in our lives. Frankly, many of us are finding that we're having to work harder and harder at it. Nevertheless, I am among those working toward reinventing a notion of freedom that even the recession can't suppress.

Here, in a nutshell, are three ways I am personally reinventing freedom in my life.

1. The freedom to find joy in my work.

I wanted to work when the researchers surveyed me several years ago—and I still want to work. If I can keep my ego out of it, I can celebrate the fact that postponing retirement was something I was choosing to do, anyway.

2. The freedom to enjoy the hours I'm not working.

Many of us are working fewer hours than we wish we could. The dollars just aren't there, and we are working temporary, freelance, part-time, or whatever. Now is our opportunity to practice hard core the simplicity we've been flirting with ever since we put books like Simple Abundance onto the best-seller lists.

3. The freedom to be a whole person, regardless of what I'm facing.

Those of you who have read my book *The Year I Saved My (Downsized) Soul: A Boomer Woman's Search for Meaning...and a Job* know that I was out of work for many months. During those months, I had to dig deep to find that place in me that knew I was going to be alright, regardless of the external challenges that I faced. This is spiritual freedom—perhaps the most precious and valuable freedom of all.

[1]Anne Fisher, "Are You Stuck in Middle Management Hell?" *Fortune*, August 15, 2006.

[2]Eileen Marcus and Carol Orsborn , "Boomer Wanted: The Next Great Workplace Revolution" (whitepaper, Fleishman-Hillard's FH Boom, November 30, 2007).

[3]"Buddy, Can You Spare a Job?" The Metlife Study of the New Realities of the Job Market for Aging Baby Boomers (report, David DeLong Associates, October 2009).

[4]Term credited to Civic Ventures: www.Encore.org.

[5]For an in-depth accounting of job loss as a rite of passage, please see Carol Orsborn, *The Year I Saved My (Downsized) Soul: A Boomer Woman's Search for Meaning...and a Job* (Louisville, KY: Vibrant Nation, 2009).

[6]Tina Brown, "The Gig Economy," *The Daily Beast*, January 12, 2009, http://www.thedailybeast.com/blogs-and-stories/2009-01-12/the-gig-economy/full/.

[7]Rich Morin, *"Take This Job and Love It": Job Satisfaction Highest among the Self-Employed*, Pew Research Center, September 17, 2009, http://pewsocialtrends.org/pubs/743/job-satisfaction-highest-among-self-employed#prc-jump.

6

PLANNING FOR
THE FUTURE:
Finances, Insurance, Real Estate, and Health-care Costs

Financial marketers who do speak to her tend to do so with confident assurances that they know what's best for her, a patronizing approach almost worse than ignoring the Vibrant Woman altogether.

The first and perhaps only thing marketers in the financial, health-care, real-estate, and insurance industries need to know about the Vibrant Woman is this: She doesn't trust you. In one of our surveys of Vibrant Women, 67 percent reported that they either trust their financial advisers and institutions less than before the recession or never trusted them in the first place.[1] And that's the good news. What is even more telling is that only 26 percent of these women have any kind of financial planner at all.[2] But don't take it personally. The Vibrant Woman has never been fully invested in the belief that either corporate and governmental institutions or their representatives would be there for her in the end.

One soundtrack of her adult life has been an accelerating drumbeat of indications that she would not be able to rely on the same level of external resources enjoyed by her parents' generation. Whereas mom and dad were rewarded for placing their trust in government, unions, and corporations watching out for their interests, the Vibrant Woman came of age in post-patriarchal times. Leading-edge Boomers lost their innocence with the triple assassinations of JFK, MLK, and RFK, while those on the trailing edge had their own defining moment: Watergate. The Vietnam War, followed by stretches of economic stagnation and periodic financial crises, including the S&L crisis, Latin American debt debacles, the tech bubble, and two recent recessions, have left Boomer women feeling that it is high time to take matters into her own hands.

Despite the liberation she sought and won in the workplace and other arenas, the Vibrant Woman's active interest in managing money is a more recent development. Previously, she generally assumed a traditional relationship with family finances, especially if she was married. At younger ages, she was also juggling other responsibilities at work and home. Financial planning often entered her life as part of her spouse's retirement planning or need for life insurance. And even if she did pay attention, she probably assumed that booms like those of the 1980s and late 1990s would lift her savings before she needed them in what seemed then like a very distant future. Besides, it would have taken a lot of initiative to pay attention to a financial industry that paid no attention to her.

TAKING THE REINS

Ironically, at the same moment that her own aging brought the need for a financial future into sharper focus, the recession crushed her retirement savings, whacked the accumulated gain in her home, and quite possibly downsized her job. Simultaneously fueled by a post-menopausal surge of renewed vigor and confronting the fact that she is most likely to outlive the man in her life, she grabbed the financial reins that her Boomer husband was all to happy to pass on. Motivated by equal parts concern and determination, she now represents 50 percent of stock investors, holds 89 percent of U.S. bank accounts, and owns half of all privately held U.S. firms. She also influences or directly handles 80 percent of all her family's financial decisions.[3]

For the post-crash Boomer couple, it is the woman who typically turns to her husband, initiating the idea of making contact with an institution or adviser with these three powerful words: "We need help." Just as she has taken charge of her family's medical care, she is using skills honed in that work to conduct research, review statements, and talk to friends about financial planning. This couple will not hire a new adviser without her approval.

If only she knew what makes for a good adviser—and good advice. In the face of an industry invested in keeping its work complicated and opaque, her version of a hiring decision can often feel like,

---

She grabbed the financial reins that her Boomer husband was all to happy to pass on.

"Whom do I mistrust the least?" Financial marketers who do speak to her do so with confident assurances that they know what's best for her, a patronizing approach almost worse than ignoring the Vibrant Woman altogether. She suspects that many fail to disclose their conflicts of interest in offering cloudy and misleading advice. *Can I rely on a high-deductible health-insurance plan? How do I really know whether I have a good deal on my mortgage or not or whether to pay it off and invest my savings elsewhere? How can I determine if life insurance is a way to save or waste money? Can I afford a second home?* Everywhere she turns, she is greeted by advisers with a vested interest in the answer they provide.

It comes as no surprise that given the dearth of objective advice, the Vibrant Woman has turned a handful of experts who hail from her own demographic, such as Jane Bryant Quinn, Alice Schroeder, and Suze Orman, into financial celebrities. Boomer women are hungry for somebody who speaks their language and will give the facts to them straight. But set against the backdrop of a financial universe that seems increasingly out of sync with her ethics and values, let alone her common sense, she is reserving the right to feel angry and confused.

Here are some of the areas in her life where the Vibrant Woman needs help to make the right financial decisions:

SAVING AND INVESTING FOR HER FUTURE[4]

The Vibrant Woman wants solid advice about how to plan for her own financial future. *How much money should I save? How should I invest it? When can I start spending it? When can I consider stopping full-time work?*

She assumes that Social Security is unreliable, private pensions are largely a thing of the past, and even Medicare might not be solvent when she needs it. At the turn of the first decade of the new millennium, she even has to wonder what happens if her bank goes under. In fact, having lost faith in the reliability of both investments and entitlements, continuing to work is her number one response to long-term concerns.

As long as they stay employed, or their parents don't have to spend all of their own savings before they die, most Vibrant Women are pretty sure they'll stay afloat. But they still worry about the vaguely conceived time somewhere down the road when they will no longer be working and need to know how to manage the unknowns. *How should I factor in inflation? What if there's another meltdown?* Am I in danger of outliving my money? Very few companies are answering these very important questions.

DIVORCE AND WIDOWHOOD

According to statistics, a Vibrant Woman who is married is likely to end up single somewhere down the road, either as a widow or divorcee. In fact, it is the woman in the couple that represents the demographic most likely to initiate a late-in-life divorce. There are growing needs for financial and legal assistance for these women, whether their divorce or widowhood leaves them well-provided for or not. *Should I keep my house? Can I afford to travel? Can I continue helping out the kids? Will I have enough money if I live to be 100?*

HEALTH-CARE COSTS

The Boomer woman has had a front row seat to the decline of health-care service coupled with its astronomical increase in cost. She's watching her parents eat away at their own savings as well as her own on health care, and she is subsidizing her grown children and grandchildren's medical expenses, as well. The health-care reform's provision to cover her children up to age 26 is an acknowledgment of current realities—but it will not help her with deductibles, noncovered expenses, and all other expenses

---

Workers between the ages of 51 and 61, even if only part-time or temporary, experience fewer major diseases and are able to function better day-to-day than people who stop working altogether.

---

long after twenty-six birthdays will have come and gone. But these realities only describe her challenges. The health-care and financial industries need to answer such questions as: *What kind of insurance should I have on myself? What should my parents be paying for their supplemental coverage? When is it OK to see a doctor out of my network? How much money and insurance am I likely to need at the very end of my life?*

We will address health and fitness in the next chapter, but those topics have a financial impact as well. One key financial strategy for the Vibrant Woman is to keep herself healthy—well enough to keep working and to avoid major medical costs in the future. In a study by the University of Maryland, it was found that workers between the ages of 51 and 61, even if only part-time or temporary, experience fewer major diseases and are able to function better day-to-day than people who stop working altogether.[5]

MULTIGENERATIONAL NEEDS: THE FULL NEST

The Vibrant Woman's burden as a mother and grandmother goes beyond bridging health-care costs for her extended family. Many Boomer women find themselves also providing significant financial support as well as housing for their grown children and grandchildren, as well as parents and in-laws. In fact, in VibrantNation.com surveys of our members, we found that in addition to health-care assistance, more than one quarter surveyed are helping adult children with housing costs (29 percent) and daily living expenses (26 percent). They also spend significant amounts on education, clothing, and toys. What is most alarming: 44 percent say that they're dipping into their own retirement fund to support their offspring.[6] Almost two-thirds of Boomers believe they don't have enough money put away for retirement.[7] Who can she rely on to help her understand how to gain a sense of security about her financial future?

INHERITANCE AND ESTATE-PLANNING

All her financial news is not bad. In spite of the recession, Boomer women will be the recipients of the largest transfer of inherited wealth in history.[8] The Vibrant Women is likely to inherit wealth from her own parents, her husband, and, through him, her parents-in-law. As these Vibrant Women come into their inheritance, they will be charged with making wise decisions about the biggest

Boomer women will be the recipients of the largest transfer of inherited wealth in history.

lump sums of money many will have seen over the course of their lives. Some will have the means to use a portion of their inheritance on discretionary spending, building additions to homes or buying new ones, buying luxury cars, and traveling to exotic places. In their 50s and 60s, these Vibrant Women will suddenly need to develop their own estate plans and philanthropy.[9] Banks, investment firms, lawyers, nonprofits, and community foundations should be working with her now to develop her capabilities as a family benefactor and philanthropist before she actually has to fill those roles.

TESTED BY THE RECESSION

As we've noted earlier, the Vibrant Woman is creative, resourceful, and resilient. She is at a stage in life where she is caring less about what others think and gaining confidence in her own ability to make

---

"We're all going to outlive our money and our husbands."

---

good decisions—financial and otherwise. For instance, in addition to figuring out new and creative ways to continue to make money, she's willing to downsize or take in boarders, if that's what it takes. As one Vibrant Woman wryly commented: "We're all going to outlive our money and our husbands. The only difference between those of us who are better off and those who are less fortunate is not whether you're going to end up sharing a house with roommates, but how many people you're going to be sharing your bathroom with."

BREAKING THROUGH THE WALL OF MISTRUST

All these reasons make the Vibrant Woman a potentially lucrative client for marketers in the financial, real-estate, health-care, and insurance fields. In fact, given her pervasive lack of faith in institutions across the board, whoever breaks through the wall of distrust first to provide her with real solutions and/or at least ameliorate her anxiety, will have precious little competition for her sizable business.

While she hasn't found the supplier yet, she's pretty sure there's some resource out there that has the information she needs to make the most out of what she has managed to save, the entitlements she's owed, and the money she will earn and inherit. She would love to know more about long-term care insurance, Medicare Advantage HMOs, variable annuities, reverse mortgages, longevity insurance, trust funds, and many of the innovative products and services marketers have to offer. But having been burned by venerable

---

Sooner or later she'd still better place her bet or she's going to be left behind.

---

brands and advisers in the past, she's savvy enough to be asking tougher questions this time around. This includes turning up the heat on both the institutions themselves and their foot soldiers: the wealth and insurance advisers, bankers, CPAs, consultants, traders, brokers, realtors, coaches, salespeople, and representatives. She wants to know whether she is truly getting independent, informed counsel or if the pitch she's receiving—no matter how persuasively delivered—has been tainted by vested interests and/or fine-print disclaimers. She will check on whether the investment is FDIC-insured, what assurances she has that promises will be kept, whether the rules are going to change, and if the company will still be around in twenty years.

Given the current climate of distrust, the challenge for marketers to make peace with her may seem insurmountable. It's not. She is, above all, a realist. In a complex world in which even Alan Greenspan admits to having been stumped, she is already factoring in her assessment that the game is at the very least complex and may very well be rigged. Nevertheless, she realizes that sooner or later she'd still better place her bet or she's going to be left behind.

IMPLICATIONS FOR MARKETERS

Some brands and advisers are doing a better job connecting with Vibrant Women than others. Here are some key points for marketers to consider.

Don't confuse her with her parents. Ironically, the better the pitch and style that worked with her parents, the least likely it is going to succeed with her. On the most basic level, wear a suit and tie, call her Mrs., and tell her not to worry about a thing, and she'll head for the exit. Brands and advisers who turn the old paradigms upside down are the ones who will be most likely to win her trust.

> **Engage her in dialogue.** This is not a woman who just wants you to tell her what to do. What she craves, instead, is to establish an authentic relationship with you and your organization. Think about being in dialogue with her rather than having all the answers. After all, you don't really know how long she's going to live, whether she's going to stay healthy and for how long, whether her parents will have anything left in the end, and so on. Neither do you know how changes in corporate and government entitlements, inflation, the real-estate market, and the uncharted future performance of most investments are going to impact her financial picture.

> **Be authentic.** This means you come from a place of willingness to acknowledge your own vulnerabilities, doubts, and questions, as well as listening to hers. In place of promises built on sand, you deliver your guidance centered in the best you have to offer: informed, up-to-date intelligence. Key to this is the transparent presentation of both the pros and cons of your suggestions along with making alternatives and options crystal clear.

> **Let her make up her own mind.** She's a grown-up. Trust her to consider the truth about the risks and benefits and to make a decision she can live with. Caveat: You'd better know your stuff and be up on the latest, or she'll be taking her business elsewhere.

> **Don't make assurances you can't deliver on.** Remember, she is listening to the news, doing independent research, and has arrived at your portal skeptical about your brand and you in the first place. That means that both institutions and their representatives have to tell the truth about the boundaries of their knowledge. We are living in uncertain times, and if you make promises she knows you can't keep, she will look elsewhere for guidance. And keep in mind: she is reading the fine print. If the disclaimer at the bottom of the ad, brochure, or website reverses the assurances you make in the headline above, she will take note.

> **Tell her what you will do for her, not how rock solid you are.** In our post melt-down economy, in which established names like Washington Mutual and Lehman Brothers disappeared off the map, don't expect her to believe you—or even care—that your institution is rock solid, stable, and has a hundred-year-old history. She is far less concerned about what a venerable institution you are than what you can do for her. And in this regard, she is far more interested in the facts about the products and services you offer than she is in your organization's mission statement.

> **Listen to learn what is motivating her.** As we reported in the last chapter, she's not thinking about going on a never-ending vacation with or without pina colada in hand. In fact, a recent study shows that the number one concern aging consumers share is simply to not be a burden to their children. In fact, the survey reveals respondents to be over five times more worried about the possibility of becoming a burden than the possibility of dying.[10] The most important question you can ask a Vibrant Woman is this: *"What are you hoping your planning for the future will allow you to achieve?"*

> **Don't use photographs of her resting her head on her husband's shoulder.** Don't expect her to resonate with pictures of men playing rounds of golf or fly-fishing, and, for heaven's sake, don't portray a man her husband's age in a romantic relationship with a much younger woman.

The Voices of Vibrant Nation

"Medicare and Social Security may be leaking, but at least you've got a seat. Well, at least for the time being. The relief could be brief, because there are mighty forces trying to torpedo the life boats."

ON ANXIETY ABOUT THE FUTURE
BLOG BY SUSAN SWARTZ, "JUICY TOMATOES"

Vibrant Woman are worried about the future of Medicare and Social Security. Talk of any changes are perceived by many as a serious breach of trust.

Bad economic times color one's perspective on many things. Suddenly it's not so bad to be getting older. The worst recession in eighty years can make a person grateful to have lived long enough to climb into one or two life boats. Medicare and Social Security may be leaking, but at least you've got a seat.

Well, at least for the time being. The relief could be brief, because there are mighty forces trying to torpedo the life boats. Opponents of Social Security and Medicare would like to undo both, leave it to individuals to find their own best deals. Critics, including members of Congress, sneer at these government guarantees like they're some kind of public assistance. They call them entitlements. But wait a minute. Social Security and Medicare are no more entitlements than members of Congress get with their own socialized health insurance, made in the United States.

For us regular people, they're a return on our long-time investments. We've had money taken from our paychecks for Medicare and Social Security ever since we started working. It's been our deal with the government that there'd be this sure thing when we needed it.

Not that it's enough. You have to buy a supplement if you want more than bare-bones Medicare. And Social Security is a nice allowance, but you can't live on it. Most people expect to also rely on their greater savings, investments, and pension. But look what's happened to them. No sure thing there, either. Plenty of retirees turn around and go back to work.

When I asked in a bookstore for books on retirement, the clerk, in gray ponytail and Birkenstocks, said, "Who can afford to retire?" I'm starting to worry that he might be right. Maybe we need to change the lyrics in the song from "I hope I die before I get old," to "I hope I die before I go broke."

ON SHOWING HER THE BOTTOM LINE
FROM A CONVERSATION ON VN

Vibrant Women are educated and vocal in assigning blame to those who they perceive as having betrayed their confidence.

Hedda:

I have to write this quickly, so excuse the possible errors. I have an undergrad in economics (and 2 masters), and here is my take on it.... There was, as always w/ humans, a bit of greed involved with all this. With any corporate/bank venture, it is all about the money—show me the bottom line. The United States was booming (before George W.), and banks were loaning money on homes with very little money down (3 percent in some cases). It was betting on the future increase—"they knew" the prices of homes were going to rise and keep rising, thus the home would naturally build its equity. It was the time of "easy and cheap money." Any fool with some understanding of the world should have known this good time could not go on forever. There was full employment and good salaries. Folks were buying their biggest item (a home) with little money down and then charging the furniture and appliances on their credit cards at whopping rates. Oh boy...somehow the reality of the real "value" of the home would have to become concrete—home prices were inflated, Americans were deep in debt, the wars were bankrupting the treasury, yadda yadda. How did everyone think we were going to foot the bill of the war? If you borrow from Peter to pay Paul, eventually Peter will want his due also. Folks were simply "house poor" with payments they could not keep up with when the layoffs came....America was in debt up to her ears...And OH, oops the walls came crumbling down. In the past (I am 60) one could purchase a home only with a substantial (20-percent) down payment—and you had to qualify with a substantial income. In addition, we did not have all that credit card debt adding to the problem. What happened was a bit of banking greed, but also a bit of our material culture greed in "wanting everything and wanting it now"...remember Willy Wonka and the Chocolate Factory and the spoiled girl? Oh and by the way, if you think the President can fix this in ONE YEAR you need an education to understand all this mess takes TIME—he cannot wave a magic wand and do away with eight years of mistakes, sorry. There needs to be a bit of accountability experienced by people who just may have gotten in over their heads in purchases counting on only the good times and not realizing the ups and downs of a market economy and the significance of saving for that rainy day (and the layoff).

ON NOT GETTING FOOLED
VN INTERVIEW WITH AUTHOR JANE BRYANT QUINN*

"Objective, intelligent financial advisers can be hard to find because most financial advisers sell products. This means they make their living by selling you a product that carries a commission—and the higher the commission, the better...Fee-only financial advisers are the advisers that I recommend."

Objective, intelligent financial advisers can be hard to find because most financial advisers sell products. This means they make their living by selling you a product that carries a commission — and the higher the commission, the better. This is what makes various tax-deferred annuity products so popular in the market. They are very high-commission products. So are the managed accounts offered by brokerage firms, in which the managers select mutual funds or stocks for you. All the brokerage accounts are moving in this direction because they need the high commissions to succeed. They try to accumulate assets from people, put them into packaged accounts, and say, "You don't need to think about it any more. We have the best people." Here are my guidelines for choosing a financial adviser:

A high commission is never OK.

So many people don't know what else to do. They think, "Everyone's putting their money in this firm, and it's a big company with an established name, so it must be OK." But if it's a high commission, it's never OK.

Find a fee-only financial adviser.

Some financial planners don't sell products. Instead, they charge you purely for their advice. If you want them to manage your money, they charge you 1 percent for money management, and they put your money into no-load (no commission) mutual funds. These fee-only financial advisers are the advisers that I recommend.

Check out the National Association of Personal Financial Planners (NAPFA).

This is one place where you can find fee-only financial planners.

Or try Garrett Planning Network.com.

Garrett Planning Network is another such resource. They work very much with middle income people and have only one fee—they charge only fees for their advice.

Don't be fooled by "fee-based advisers."

Some advisers who charge commissions try to look like fee-only advisers by calling themselves "fee-based advisers." Don't be confused. A fee-based adviser is still selling a product, whether it's a packaged mutual fund account or an annuity. You want a fee-only adviser, and you will know it because, in fact, there are no commissions on the product he or she sells.

*Jane Bryant Quinn, *Making the Most of Your Money Now* **(New** York: Simon & Schuster, 2009).

ON SELF-RELIANCE
FROM A CONVERSATION ON VN

"I think group homes or sharing expenses and home responsibilities with someone are interesting alternatives. Anyone exploring this?"

Theboomerbomb:

I am 60, single, no children. I have worked most of my life earning a six-plus figure income for the last fifteen years of my corporate life. I found that the more money I earned, the more work and worry consumed my life. Can anyone relate? However, having a comfortable financial security and the time to enjoy it can be a difficult balance in today's world of unstable markets, inflation, and two to five more years of recession. The consensus is two to five years by the economists I read, but everyone agrees, they don't really know. So where does that leave us? [...]

I think a lot of us are in the same leaky boat whether we believe it or not. I am one health crisis away from losing my house and small assets. I don't trust the stock market or real estate for investment because of the time required to make it work...I think group homes or sharing expenses and home responsibilities with someone are interesting alternatives. Anyone exploring this?

Wendy1958:

The idea of a financial plan in the current state of society is fast becoming an obsolete idea. It's time to get creative and think outside the arena of retirement plans. Many people are losing all they have set aside for retirement, and the value of money as it exists is fast disappearing. [...] The social security system is almost dead. In a very few short years, it won't exist. In light of that, I would like to gather with other like-minded people and move into a more tribal-type living situation. It's either doing that or working until I drop. I prefer the former as it allows for a better quality of life.

SassySenior:

"We are now considering purchasing or building a property designed as a family compound that will include me, my two children, the grandchildren, and my children's in-laws if they like—everyone will have private quarters, including kitchens, but some areas will be common, and we're even considering decreasing the number of vehicles (and attendant insurance costs). And in these uncertain times, it could be that families will return to

135

multigenerational housing. There are also unrelated individuals banding together, pooling resources, and buying or renting much superior housing than any of them could afford as individuals.[...] If this country sees super inflation as a result of our economic crisis, you will be seeing some interesting changes—and possibly some for the better.

ON IRRATIONAL OPTIMISM

BLOG BY SARAH GAYLE CARTER, "SARAH GAYLE CARTER'S JOURNAL"

"I'd be lying if I said the recession hasn't affected my plans and my outlook. When I first decided to sell my house in Richmond, it was because I wanted to simplify my life, but by the time the "for sale" sign went up in my yard, I realized I couldn't afford to stay there even if I wanted to...The recession has changed the stage set I'd cast for my own personal play, but I still feel optimistic about the future."

In the short time since I started this journal, the United States has fallen into the worst economic crisis we've seen in seventy years. Last June, when I began telling my story, it felt like I was embarking on an exciting new adventure—and in most respects, I still feel that way. But I'd be lying if I said the recession hasn't affected my plans and my outlook.

When Russ and I first got together, we talked about his lifelong dream of living in Italy. One of the first questions he asked was, "If this works out with us, would you share the dream?" I responded with an enthusiastic "Yes!" Now, I don't know if that will ever be possible. It would require selling the farm, and, as we all know, real estate just isn't very liquid right now. As beautiful as the farm is, it's off the beaten path—mid-coast Maine, near but not on the water. Clearly not the moment to sell—at least not with any expectation of the kind of price this magical place ought to bring. So, though we sometimes indulge in a little virtual real-estate shopping in cyber space, we're resigned to socking in here on the farm for the foreseeable future. After all, it's a very special place, and we're lucky to be here.

But, dreams of Italy aside, the real issue of the moment for me hits closer to the bone.

I never had much personal money to begin with. When I had to close my design business because it wasn't doing well, I took a leap of faith—believing that I could support a scaled-down lifestyle by painting and doing other odd-and-end jobs. When I first decided to sell my house in Richmond, it was because I wanted to simplify my life—but by the time the "for sale" sign went up in my yard, I realized I couldn't afford to stay there even if I wanted to. In the middle of my deliberations about what plan B might look like, the focus shifted to Maine. I would live with Russ and felt confident that I could generate at least enough income to take care of myself. Maintaining some degree of autonomy was important to me. For a while it seemed to be working.

Then came fall and the first waves of financial collapse. Commissions dried up. How many people are going to order dog portraits when they're worried about paying their mortgage? Precious few. So I've had to come to grips with the fact that I may not have even the small-scale financial independence I assumed I could maintain. Italy is out for the immediate future, and Russ and I are living on pretty limited means—at least until the real-estate market turns around.

The prospect of being financially dependent again after so many years on my own is disconcerting. I came into my relationship with Russ expecting that I would have enough income to at least handle my own personal overhead, as well as contribute in some way to our household by buying food or whatever. But all of a sudden I had to say to Russ, "You know, I'm not sure how long I can keep this up, and it's making me nervous. I don't want you to resent me." I remember from my first marriage, how it felt to have to ask my husband for money to go to the grocery store. It was horrible. Humiliating. […]

The recession has changed the stage set I'd cast for my own personal play, but I still feel optimistic about the future. I'm in a relationship that feels solid and loving and makes me happy. Russ and I are healthy. We have our children. We can hang out at the farm and eat potatoes if we have to. That doesn't sound like a scary picture to me. We have the things that are important.

My optimism isn't based on a delusion that things will go back to what they were before. I just happen to believe that somehow Russ and I, and all of us, can patch things together, make do, and be happy. I've learned the hard way that real optimism has less to do with what happens to you in your life than how you handle it. You meet what comes and play the cards you're dealt. In the end, happiness isn't determined by outside circumstances, but rather by an inner condition. An attitude that, when trouble hits, allows you to respond with, "This is interesting. I wonder what will happen next?" We can choose to be curious and open to possibilities, instead of panicked. We can choose hope.

ON LIVING WITH THE PAIN OF HEALTH-CARE COSTS
FROM A CONVERSATION ON VN

Concerns about health-care costs are on the Vibrant Woman's mind and factoring into her plans for the future.

DebbieSue:

I am afraid to retire! I do not plan to retire, in the full sense of the word. I plan to find something different to be able to bring in more of the dough to go along with the bacon that the hubby brings in. I will still have insurance through my husband's plan for a while, God fearing and the creek don't rise. But, when he and I are both retired, we will both still have to have a way of bringing in the dough and bacon. We both need medication, and I plan to try to stop taking some of what I am on in order to save some money. I have a chronic pain condition as a result of an adverse case of shingles, and my husband has had psoriatoric arthritis since age 19 and an inherited cholesterol problem where his body manufactures too much cholesterol. So, it is my plan that maybe after being a teacher for twenty-eight years, I will not have as much stress to cope with. Therefore, I will be able to tolerate the pain that I have. It makes me so angry, sad, irritated, and disappointed in our government that they have done nothing to make the cost of health care better in our country. They have turned their heads and looked the other way when the drug manufacturers began to skyrocket their prices overnight it seemed. In fact, they even let them advertise with money that they are ripping off from us, and they are not doing research as promised. They are spending 30 percent of the cost to advertising versus 14 percent of the cost to research. Research was the number one reason that they claimed that their drugs went up. To me, sometimes they are just one step above another kind of a person or organization that sells drugs—the corner drug dealer! It sickens me in a way to think that older people and single people, like single mothers, cannot even think about retiring. I guess that if you are doing something you still love to do, it is fortunate for you that you can still enjoy working. But, for many, retirement is the only thing they look forward to, and then they can do something else with their lives that they want to do. But, this hope is not even possible for some, and the biggest reason is because of health care. There has to be a change, a change to prevention is what has to happen. There are just too many people who are sick, which is causing all our health-care costs to go up. We need, as a society, to invest in positive changes. It may hurt in the beginning when we have to give up some of the things that are causing us to suffer, or it may hurt some to get off of their lazy butts to get up and exercise, but just think of how much better we all will feel in the long run and how much more we will get to do with our lives. We have to start being more positive thinkers, because this is the first place that dis-ease begins. Positive praying to change our negative thinking has to be something we all do. Our minds are taking our bodies down to the negative place our minds let us take them.

ON ENTITLEMENTS

BLOG BY CAROL ORSBORN, "INSIDE THE NATION"

Talk about "entitlements" makes Vibrant Women understandably nervous.

Entitlement: 1 a: the state or condition of being entitled : right b: a right to benefits specified especially by law or contract 2: a government program providing benefits to members of a specified group ; also : funds supporting or distributed by such a program 3: belief that one is deserving of or entitled to certain privileges.

—Merriam-Webster Online[11]

If Tarp is the first domino and the financial bailout is the second, the third in line for political/public scrutiny is sure to be "entitlements."

I really dislike this word, as I perceive it to be a loaded euphemism for Social Security. It's not the first or second definitions of entitlement, per Merriam-Webster Online, that bother me. These definitions are simply stated facts: Under the existing law, members of a specific group (in this case, people who have paid into Social Security and who reach a certain age) are provided with a benefit.

The definition also uses the word "contract." I have no problem with this, either. Those of us who work and have had no choice about if, whether, or how much to pay into the system have an agreement with the government. We concede to let the government withhold a substantial portion of the money we have earned from every single paycheck in exchange for benefits to be paid to us down the road.

I remember the very first time I received a paycheck, when I was in my early 20s. I'd been counting on every penny of my slim salary for living expenses. What a shock to see how much had been taken out for this then-too-remote-to-even-conceptualize notion of "retirement." I must admit that on some levels, the amount taken out for Social Security, taxes, health care, 401k plans, and God knows what else has never lost its shock value.

But here's the thing: I may have disliked the chunk of income that went missing from my paycheck every other week, but I never thought to question that grandma and grandpa and later mom and dad weren't deserving of their Social Security benefits. Society acknowledging the reality of physical and mental diminishments that come with age and taking care of the elderly was the reality within which our generation was raised.

So, this brings us to the third loaded definition: last on the list, but having inexorably risen to the top like curd in a bottle of sour milk. "Entitlement: Belief that one is deserving of or entitled to certain privileges."

An example of common usage, please? OK: how about "This selfish generation of Boomers believes that they deserve special privileges as their entitlement." This is the language of us vs. them: of blame and of shame.

I think you get the gist of it. For starters, what does "belief" have to do with anything? We believe in the Tooth Fairy and Santa Claus, we do not "believe" in all the money that was taken out of our paychecks to help our parents and grandparents nor do we "believe" that we have an agreement that we will receive benefits in turn.

How about the word "privilege"? Merriam-Webster to the rescue, again: "privilege: A right or immunity granted as a peculiar benefit, advantage, or favor."[12] Social Security: a favor? And finally: "deserve": "Suitable for a reward."[13] Social Security: a reward?

When we use the word "entitlement," are we really meaning to say that Social Security is a favor only to be granted as a reward for those who we believe are deserving of it? And that this understanding of this "entitlement" is a matter of taking personal advantage for one's self at the expense of others?

If so, how far the understanding of entitlements has eroded! In fact, when you read the history of Social Security, you will discover that the generation of young adults of the day was actually relieved that the traditional private burden of taking care of aging parents was going to be shared on a societal level. Social Security was as much an aid to people under 65 as it was to those who were old enough to receive benefits.

The dominos have already begun to fall, and trust me, "entitlements" are next in line. And while I don't begin to have the solution to our world's economic crisis, I do know that in regards to entitlement, there is one critical place to begin. And that is to unpack the loaded language we've taken to using, restoring fairness and respect back into the dialogue, and, regardless of our age, working together to fix this mess for the sake of all the generations.

[1]"Resilience Survey," VibrantNation.com, November 10, 2009.

[2]Lesley M. Harris, "Most Baby Boomers Don't Use Financial Planners," SBWire, February 13, 2008, http://www.sbwire.com/press-releases/sbwire-16049.htm.

[3]Cheri Kuick, "Targeting Affluent Women: How to Build Sales by Tapping the Economic Power of Women (presentation, AIG's "Why Women Are Wining" Conference, Chicago, Illinois, July 13,2008).

[4]Also known as "retirement planning." But given the lack of relevance of the phrase "retirement" as addressed previously, this is a phrase we recommend that marketers avoid.

[5]Yujie Zhan, Mo Wang, Songqi Liu, and Kenneth S. Shultz, "Bridge Employment and Retirees' Health: A Longitudinal Investigation," *Journal of Occupational Health Psychology* 14, no. 4 (2009):374-89.

[6]"Adult Child Survey," VibrantNation.com, June 15, 2009; "Full Nest Survey," VibrantNation.com, March 1, 2010.

[7]Eileen Marcus and Carol Orsborn ,"Boomer Wanted: The Next Great Workplace Revolution" (whitepaper, Fleishman-Hillard, November 30, 2007).

[8]The range is estimated to run as high as 25 trillion dollars. Allianz, "The Allianz American Legacies Study," as quoted in Marilyn Gardner, "The Greatest Generation Shares the Wealth," *Christian Science Monitor* (August 1, 2005), http://www.agewave.com/media_files/csm_.html.

[9]The Great Recession spawned an upswing in spending by the affluent on luxury goods and services. Don Lee, "Consumer Spending Trend Is a Shaky Foundation for Economic Recovery," *Los Angeles Times*, May 16, 2010. More on this in chapter 10, "The Good Life."

[10]"America Talks: Protecting Our Families' Financial Futures" (survey, Age Wave/Harris Interactive for Genworth Financial companies, April 12, 2010).

[11]*Merriam-Webster Online*, s.v. "entitlement," http://www.merriam-webster.com/dictionary/entitlement (accessed July 21, 2010).

[12]*Merriam-Webster Online*, s.v. "privilege," http://www.merriam-webster.com/dictionary/privilege (accessed July 21, 2010).

[13]*Merriam-Webster Online*, s.v. "deserve," http://www.merriam-webster.com/dictionary/deserve (accessed July 21, 2010).

7

360-DEGREE WELLNESS:

Body, Peace of Mind, and Spirit

After the last decade, not only dealing with the impact of her own aging body but the deterioration of external circumstances, the Vibrant Woman's definition of 'wellness' no longer confines itself to the pursuit of physical fitness. Rather, what she strives for is an increasing sense of safety and peace.

The Boomer woman who first aspired to the "Superwoman" model later rebelled against the idea that she could have, do, or be it all. She is now determined to use every tool in her considerable arsenal to redefine what it means to be a strong, healthy woman at age 50+. She'll have plenty of time to work it out. At 50, the Vibrant Woman likely has thirty or more years ahead of her, and she wants to live those years as fully as possible. However, even as she continues to up her game, so have her challenges grown and, with them, her understanding of what it means to be well.

Some of those challenges—like managing chronic health conditions such as osteoporosis, diabetes, or sexual, heart, and back issues—actually result from the longevity she now enjoys. But more and potentially bigger stressors are coming at her from all directions. Since the turn of the new millennium, a series of external events have violently attacked the sense of well-being among women, turning wellness from something she can create into something she struggles to maintain:

> 9/11 tore away the sense that her world is safe for her and for those she loves.

> Her nation has been at war for most of the new millennium, and the threat of terrorism has become a part of daily life.

> Climate change has gone from a theory to a fact she confronts in daily life, leaving her uncertain about the planet her children and grandchildren will inhabit.

> Her aging parents are increasingly looking to her for support and her own adult children, whether or not they've officially left the nest, remain more emotionally and financially dependent on her than she ever was on her own mother.

> The financial meltdown that began in 2008 undid her expectations of what the future holds for her and her family.

Women feel an innate connectedness to the lives of others and to the lives of their country and planet. After the last decade, not only

---

9/11 tore away the sense that her world is safe for her and for those she loves.

---

dealing with the impact of her own aging body but the deterioration of external circumstances, the Vibrant Woman's definition of "wellness" no longer confines itself to the pursuit of physical fitness. Rather, what she strives for is an increasing sense of safety and peace.

As a result, managing stress has become the most important way that Vibrant Women seek wellness. We're not just talking about yoga and meditation here, although those are certainly tools in her arsenal of coping strategies. The Vibrant Women, ever self-reliant, is calling on her own proactive management skills and is seeking the best possible partners and tools to help her bring that stress under control.

WELLNESS IS EVERYWHERE—OR AT LEAST SHE HOPES SO

While we will address the Vibrant Women's approach to medicine later in this chapter, it should be obvious that wellness means a lot more than "health" and involves every aspect of a woman's life-style. Taking a 360-degree view of health, the Vibrant Woman builds wellness products and services into virtually every aspect of life, from the ergonomic seat at her desk to the organic coloring she puts in her hair. In chapter 4, we noted her interest in technical fashion that offers both function and style, sleepwear that wicks away sweat from hot flashes, and leggings that improve her circulation. Companies like General Mills with its Fiber One brand and Frito-Lay with its True North snacks are offering her healthier food, and she is willing to pay more for functional foods with vitamins and probiotic cultures. Marketers need to satisfy her goal to make everything she buys and does part of her wellness routine.

WEIGHT AND FITNESS

Almost all women share at least one common measure of physical wellness: their weight. But weight is more often a source of stress than peace. Vibrant Women learn that finding some kind of peace with weight, either by reaching a weight they can maintain or accepting the weight they are, is required before they can make the most of their years after 50. At VibrantNation.com we see every variation of the mid-life woman's attitude about weight, but we don't see any women who don't think about it at all.

The Vibrant Woman has always embraced the importance of staying fit, both physically and mentally. She got her post-pregnancy body in shape with Jane Fonda or Jazzercise and was the first generation of women to wear pink ribbons as she walked for breast cancer and other causes. Even if she's not training for the Iron Man, she's joining health clubs and fitness classes in unprecedented numbers.[1]

Her athletic life-style makes her a health-care pioneer, too. Sports injuries, stemming from jogging, tennis, aerobics, hiking, and more, have become the number two reason (just behind the common cold) for a Boomer to visit a doctor's office.[2] Ironically, it is her very commitment to her health that has driven markedly increased demand for knee and hip replacements as well as treatments for plantar fasciitis, among a host of medical treatments. Even when

Even if she's not training for the Iron Man,
she's joining health clubs and fitness classes
in unprecedented numbers.

her body lets her know it's had enough, she doesn't give up. She'll transition to something kinder and gentler, like Pilates, yoga, or t'ai chi, or the latest newcomers to the workout scene, Latin-dance-inspired Zumba, Qi Gong, Wii Fit, or Nia, which combines the dance, martial, and healing arts in easy-on-the-joints movements.

She may also want to work out her brain, and an increasing number of Boomer women are using cognitive exercises to maintain mental alertness and avoid anticipated declines. Whether she plays Sudoko, uses cognitive fitness games on the Web, or buys brain games from Nintendo, the Vibrant Woman will do whatever she can to keep her mind sharp.

MEDICINE AND THE "DIFFICULT" PATIENT

When it comes to earning her trust, medical institutions rarely fare better than their counterparts in the financial world. Doctors and hospitals who found such receptive patients in her mother and father often seem at a loss to explain why the Boomer woman is so intent on being "difficult." The fact is that while her mother obediently complied with doctor's orders, the Vibrant Woman wants to be taken seriously as an equal partner in every step of the health-care process. By the time she enters the waiting room, she will already have done her own research and equipped herself with opinions, often gathered on-line, about the diagnosis, preferred treatment, and outcome. And if she doesn't like what traditional medicine has to offer, she is more than willing to go as far afield as necessary to explore alternatives. This may include everything from unlicensed acupuncture, herbal remedies, and surgery conducted overseas to exotic healing rituals in the Himalayan foothills.

Her proactive stance does not end with diagnosis and treatment. She expects to be treated well, too. The same generation of women that drove the rise of the destination spa industry wants the same kind of pampering in her medical care. Whenever she can, she is willing to pay for it. In fact, she is a prime driver behind boutique and elite health-care initiatives and will continue to bring her considerable resources to bear to get what she wants.

When she does get time with the experts, she will listen carefully, but she will also question and she will argue. If she doesn't like how she's being treated, she will take her business elsewhere. This is no small matter, given that the Vibrant Woman is the "Chief Health Officer" and the driving decision maker behind health care for herself, her husband, and many of her older and younger family members.

The Vibrant Woman's approach to medicine at this stage of life was formed by what can be the most prolonged and confusing physical experience of her life: menopause. Menopause is the crucible upon which her approach to medicine was reset. If she didn't distrust the medical establishment already, menopause

---

If she doesn't like how she's being treated, she will take her business elsewhere.

---

usually gave her good reason to do so. Who will tell her the truth about hormone replacement therapy (HRT) when her OB/GYN may not even talk to her about bioidentical hormones? She knows that Suzanne Somers wants the best for her, but why should she be forced to rely on a sitcom star for medical advice?

MEDICAL TREATMENT AS LIFE CHOICE

While the process of peri-menopause eventually comes to an end, its aftereffects on bone density, sexual health, drier skin, and thinning hair continue for even the healthiest woman. When she seeks attention and support for menopause and related medical conditions that make her moodier than she wants to be, she gets that the male and youth-oriented medical establishment just wants her to go away. She is left largely on her own to deal with the various options and weigh the benefits and costs. How aggressively she will fight the aging process— and the level of risk she is willing to take— become a matter of life choice for her.

The notion of medicine as a difficult life choice is underscored when it comes to cosmetic surgery. In many circles of Vibrant

---

In many circles, having "a little work done" is the norm.

Women—particularly those in industries where competition from younger colleagues is high—having "a little work done" is the norm rather than the exception. But for every woman who undergoes the knife for a facelift or breast reduction or takes a needle for Botox injections, there are many more who opt for less invasive alternatives. Sales of antiaging products have nearly doubled over the past five years, estimated by NPD Group to be in the range of $2 billion.

Among the liveliest conversations at VibrantNation.com are the ones in which members debate the pros and cons of various moisturizers, products for thinning hair, diet remedies, lubricants, and facial hair. In lieu of trustworthy advice from designated experts, Vibrant Women turn to one another and the embarrassment-free anonymity of the social network environment to surface their concerns and to seek and offer advice.

REVISITING THE ROOT QUESTION

The Vibrant Woman's continuum of wellness practices blurs the line between the physical and the spiritual and goes to the very core of her being. In chapter 4's discussion of fashion and beauty, we traced her search for meaning to the question: "How can I regain mastery over a body that has spun out of control?" When viewing this root question through the lens of health and wellness, the call for philosophical introspection is that much more acute. Because there are no medical answers to the question regarding when to fight and when to accept the aging process, both in regards to cosmetic and medical impact, spirituality is as important a tool in her wellness arsenal as is fitness, research, alternative, and preventative care.

Her abundant spiritual resources lie just beneath the surface of her day-to-day wellness management. While she remains part of the healthiest generation of women in history, she is well aware that she, herself, is not exempt from physical setbacks. Her 360-degree approach to wellness means that she also understands that it is her choice to make physical challenges a source of either victimhood or growth, and she would prefer growth. When she becomes ill, she doesn't think of herself as a victim and prefers not to identify with her diseases and ailments. Unlike her mother's generation, she seeks to avoid guilt or shame about illness and knows from her own history that dealing with setbacks can, in fact, make her emotionally and spiritually stronger.

Relying on spiritual strength, Vibrant Women report that they have become more adept at handling the challenges life brings their way. In our survey of Vibrant Women regarding their response to difficult times, 80 percent reported that "the older I get, the more resilient I become."[3]

SPIRITUALITY AND WELLNESS

Where she once held the goal of controlling everything that happens to her, she has evolved a different understanding of what it means to be strong. According to our survey, eight out of ten respondents identify with the attitude that: "I am flexible and adaptable and make the most out of life regardless of the obstacles that come my way." The majority add: "I might influence the things that happen to and for me, but the ultimate outcome is in God's hands."

The dynamic nature of this woman's evolving spiritual beliefs is in keeping with the convergence of globalization and technology during the course of her lifetime. Hers was the first generation of women to have had access to spiritual texts from eras and regions previously regarded as "secret knowledge." Many compounded their studies with the mélange of psychology and self-improvement known as "the consciousness movement." If she didn't actually go to a training like EST or Lifespring (but many did), she went to a twelve-step program, hired a therapist or life coach, or, at the very least, turned on the TV and got her psycho-spiritual education direct from Oprah and Eckhart Tolle. Travel and the Internet have accelerated her access to the esoteric, whether it means reliving vision quests in Arizona or downloading prayers from Africa. In America, of course, spiritual offerings usually turn in to big business, and well-meaning leaders have created no end of spiritual offerings, from Byron Katie's *The Work* (it's all in how we see it) to *The Secret* (you can shape your own destiny).

The Boomer women who drove demand for new age religions continue to take their inspiration primarily from sources outside of organized religion. While they do make up a large percentage of churchgoers, they defy outdated "church lady" stereotypes that limit their spirituality to good works and cooking casseroles. In our

---

44 percent of Vibrant Women are turning
to sources other than organized religion for
spiritual guidance.

---

survey, we found that 44 percent of Vibrant Women are turning to
sources other than organized religion (books, speakers, coaches, and
workshops) for spiritual guidance. Only 23 percent find inspiration
from their current religious community and only 8 percent from the
religious community in which they were raised.[4]

Their faith in the authority of organized religion has slipped
significantly, but not their belief in God. A study by AARP found
that 94 percent of all respondents 50+ believe in God, and
interestingly enough, the higher the income, the less afraid of death
they are.[5] As clear-eyed as she is optimistic, the Vibrant Woman
knows that the jury is still out in terms of how long, let alone how
well, she will live. With health care and Medicare under siege and
with stressors ranging from a deteriorating environment to terrorist
threats on her mind, she is not so sure she will ever actually reap
the promise of her unprecedented longevity. But God knows that
she's going to try.

IMPLICATIONS FOR MARKETERS

Many hospitals and health-care providers realize that the
Boomer woman is their most important target, but you
wouldn't know it from the way they market themselves.
Here are a few pointers for them and others:

> **Don't be afraid of a spiritual angle in your messaging.**
You may feel like mentioning faith or spirituality is inappropriate,
but used in the right way, it will appeal to almost every Boomer
woman.

> **Recognize that wellness means safety, for her and those she loves.** While she wants to be fit (and almost always wants to weigh less), her primary goal is not mastering her physical conditions. Rather, she is taking a 360-degree view that embraces external as well as internal factors.

> **Just because the Vibrant Woman isn't happy about the physical effects of aging doesn't mean she can't laugh at them.** Use humor to explain your offer. But take care that she doesn't think you're laughing at her. One of the best tools in your kit is to use the voice of one of her peers, a "woman like her" to illustrate or comment on conditions and circumstances, only one of her own would fully understand.

> **Consider addressing aging directly.** Women themselves aren't confused about the impact of aging on their bodies and which new products and devices offer attractive ways to address the conditions that come with age. Don't make the mistake of bundling these offerings under the banner "senior," however. She won't identify. Rather, drug chains should consider an aisle devoted to "age-relief" products that offer straightforward solutions without condescension or embarrassment.

> **Keep in mind, Vibrant Women are more active than you think.** They are tired of seeing themselves depicted passively, strolling fully clothed on beaches or sitting on docks. You don't need to show her climbing to the top of the mountain or skydiving to get the message across, either. She's living a full, rich life every day, and the images advertisers use to appeal to her should reflect her full level and range of engagement.

> **Go where she is—whether it's the yoga studio, the writing class, the investing seminar— and let her try your products firsthand.** The Boomer woman is wary about being told what to do and what to use. You will earn more from getting her to

sample your product on her own, and then trust that she will tell her friends.

> **Realize that it's all connected.** We use the phrase "360-degree wellness" because it involved every aspect of the Vibrant Woman's life. For her, diet is connected to faith, and faith is connected to her love of friends and family. Your product or service is not part of an isolated category but a key to her successfully managing a healthy life.

The Voices of Vibrant Nation

The Vibrant Woman arrives at the portal of medical care already armed with information. Unlike her mother's generation, she will question authority and argue with the experts.

ON ACCEPTANCE VERSUS "FIGHTING IT"
FROM A CONVERSATION ON VN

The Vibrant Woman has to decide for herself whether and to what degree she is going to intervene with the organic processes of aging. For many, the jury is still out.

Dallas Lady:

I have a friend who is trying to do this. (Use hormonal therapy to delay the onset of menopause.) For the life of me, I really don't understand why. She has had to deal with painful enlarged ovaries reacting to the hormones, and I wonder if this is preferable to entering menopause? I'm not saying that menopause is a cakewalk—but neither was adolescence. I am saying that our bodies are doing exactly what they are supposed to do in this case, so why fight it to that degree?

I'm not saying we should purposefully face pain or that we shouldn't do what we can to feel our best—within reason. But I also wouldn't do Botox. I'll just take care of what I have naturally and hope for the best and face my future as naturally as I can as God, nature, or someone intended.

Buzzingbee:

My gender doesn't come from a period, it comes from my brain. I am a beautiful, young 61. My vagina has not dried. I am sexy (have younger men asking me out, not realizing I am married), and any foggy thinking is going to happen to anyone at some point in their life, more likely the more chemicals they take. Since I'm 5' tall and weigh 100 pounds, I'm not worried about that; I do a lot of walking. To my way of thinking, periods are for childbearing not femininity.

Latebloomer57:

Now that I am on the other side of it (haven't had a cycle since sometime in 2008) I love it. I've never felt so free. I don't have to worry about accidents and floods or any of that. The hot flashes aren't as bad as they used to be, and I wouldn't trade this freedom for all the eggs in the henhouse.

Maat45:

My natural cycles had ended as and when nature intended, and I never had any desire to prolong them with additives. So I'm getting older...that will happen regardless, chronologically.... The rest...emotionally, intellectually, mentally...that is entirely up to me and my attitude/philosophy. I know I am aging, but I believe, and have been told, I am doing it gracefully.

LynnetteS:

I have to say that preventing menopause sounds like preventing puberty. Menopause is not a disease, although I do concur that it can freaking feel like one sometimes.

ON SELF-ACCEPTANCE
BLOG BY SARAH GAYLE CARTER, "SARAH GAYLE CARTER'S JOURNAL"

Even if a Vibrant Woman chooses not to undergo plastic surgery herself, she is usually sympathetic to those who do.

We often hear women talk about a transition from control to acceptance happening when they turn 50, and it's true. It happened to me. [...] I had always lived under the illusion that there were infinite choices to be made and endless possibilities. I was going to lose the weight I always meant to. Everyone has a list like this, right? You can live a long time feeling like it's all possible. But a time does come when you finally get that it's not necessarily so. You have to look at yourself in the mirror and go, "This is me. This is my life. I'm 50 or 55, and my body doesn't look like it did when I was 25—and it's never going to again."

I've heard that cosmetic surgery peaks for women in their 40s. I suppose many women in their 50s must have it done too, and I'm not arguing against it, but I think among women over 50 there is a lot more of the sense that, "Well, these are my hips"—a simple acceptance of ourselves as we are. I really want to live the rest of my life with that kind of grace. I want the grace to have gray hair, to have some of my body hang or droop. Why do we women continually measure ourselves against what we looked like when we were 30? It's brutal, and we do it to ourselves. I'm not immune to this, but it's something I want to work on, consciously. I want to work on my whole life this way, thoughtfully and deliberately. It's why I want my house to be small and simple. I want to strip away the things that I only thought I needed and fill my life with the things that really matter.

ON FACING HER BIGGEST FEAR
BLOG BY BONNIE MCFARLAND, "SAVORING YOUR SIXTIES"

Many Vibrant Women are less afraid of dying than they are of meaninglessness.

What is most people's biggest fear?

You might think it's fear of dying. Or, if you've taken speaking classes, you might have heard it's fear of public speaking.

But research done by Richard Leider, author of Power of Purpose (San Francisco: Berrett-Koehler Publishers, 1997), revealed people's #1 fear to be having lived a meaningless life.

Death itself doesn't seem as frightening to us as not having fully lived our own unique lives.

We fear we'll go to our grave having never made our mark, never "sung our song."

We want to "rage against the dying of the light" as Dylan Thomas wrote, by having created a light of our own that illuminates the way for others.

Could this be your biggest fear? Deep beneath the day-to-day concerns and worries about the future, could you really be most afraid of a life without meaning?...

Discover and do what really matters to you, make the difference you want to make in the world so these will be exciting, fulfilling, and joyous years. Maybe even the best years of your life!

ON 360-DEGREE WEIGHT LOSS
FROM A CONVERSATION ON VN

Beneath issues of wellness, including weight loss, lie questions about the meaning of life.

PatB:

"Loved reading the posts and so connected to the deeper "want" beneath them all. I have very definite feelings and viewpoints about weight loss and weight regain. They go hand in hand and are beautifully played by the diet industry to keep us perpetual customers. Once I realized this, I approached weight loss differently. I'm interested only in permanent weight loss. Don't care about diets and food plans and cleansers, and things like that. IMO, that's why many of us still struggle. We're concentrating on the PHYSICAL aspect of weight—diet and exercise. This is what doctors, nutritionists, trainers, etc. are taught—the physical part. It is NOT ONLY about the physical. Permanent weight loss requires change on deeper levels of our being: mental, emotional, and spiritual.

I completely agree when people said they looked back and their pictures from high school, or their twenties, were fine! Yes, they were. Life before dieting is always preferable. Dieting only brings an obsession with food, a focus on control, and more weight. If any of us can do something good today, find a teen and get her happy about her exact size and shape right now. If we can prevent young women from taking this path of restriction/dieting and help her accept and love herself, our future health will be better for it.

My own weight loss occurred between 1996 and 2000, and in March, I'll celebrate 10 years at my current weight. I lost over 70 pounds. It's gone, folks, and it ain't coming back. I know it won't because I changed; it wasn't just my weight that changed. I want to tell you—there is no wagon. You aren't on or off, good or bad, fat or thin. You just are. If you've got to leap onto a wagon, you're being dragged away from yourself and no healing can occur there.

So, I encourage every one of you to get to the root of this. Forget food plans for a while and look inside. What's your weight doing FOR you? Giving you an excuse? Diverting you from a bad situation/job/ relationship? Soothing emotions you can't handle alone? Giving you a feeling of "freedom"? It's doing something positive for you or you wouldn't be doing it. You're at a crossroads. You can do what you've always done or take another path!"

ON PSYCHO-SPIRITUAL EMPOWERMENT
VN INTERVIEW WITH DR. CHRISTIANE NORTHRUP*

Vibrant Women are open to shifting psychological and spiritual perspectives, if it will help them avoid thinking of themselves as victims to physical issues.

"I put together a new way of thinking about the physical body based on the fullness of women's stories and how, by changing their characteristic thoughts and beliefs and victimization patterns, they really could have vibrant health. That was the missing piece of the puzzle: women's underlying mental and emotional patterns.

I've dedicated my life to everything that can go right with the female body and how to magnify that, how to sustain it, how to support it in a culture that, by and large, supports everything but. Being depressed, victimized, poor, and angry is a slam dunk. Just turn on the TV; you've got a global support network for that. So many of us live from emergency to emergency, exhausting ourselves for the things that are worth dying for, the internalized masculine.

We need to consciously choose the route of pleasure, the route of health. It takes enormous discipline to practice this. What I tell people is that if it feels pleasurable, if it will be fun, then that's how I know that it will uplift me and that I can help the endeavor. I'm interested in the organic garden model of life: you replenish the soil and the plants are healthy. This new way of thinking is what will enable women to turn around what's going on in their bodies and their lives and prevent problems in the future."

*Dr. Christiane Northrup, *The Secret Pleasures of Menopause* (Carlsbad, CA; Hay House, 2008).

ON FINDING FAITH OUTSIDE ORGANIZED RELIGION
FROM A CONVERSATION ON VN

The Vibrant Woman perceives a direct connection between her spirituality and the healthiest possible relationship to her life.

River 11283:

What I find so heartening in these responses is the demand for a practical spirituality. Whether it is found in or out of an institution, by oneself or in a group, this demand is going to be pushing toward a new way of thinking, doing, and living—more spiritually based thinking as opposed to materially based.

I read—a lot—about the growing demand for spirituality, where our churches are going, healing and prayer, and the global current of spiritual thinking. These responses really reflect a huge current of thought: turning away from the institution of religion to the more personal journey with an intimate spirituality.

I have always felt that spirituality is the root of who we are and our understanding of spirituality forms the baseline of one's life. It follows that as more and more people demand authenticity from their spiritual lives, this transforms our society and our world from a limited material basis to a more infinite spiritual basis.

As women, as spiritual thinkers, and coming into our wisdom years, we are actually creating this shift.

[…I also think that what we believe in and live out in our lives is not only more powerful to stir inspiration but stirs up more compassionate actions and more honest relations, and this will result in better health for our bodies, our families, our communities, and our nations.]

[1]Kate Arcieri, "Baby Boomers Create Boomlet at Health Clubs around Country," *The Annapolis Capital*, March 28, 2007.

[2]Bill Pennington, "Baby Boomers Stay Active, and So Do Their Doctors," *The New York Times*, April 16, 2007.

[3]"Resilience Survey," VibrantNation.com, November 10, 2009, http://www.vibrantnation.com/assets/2087/resilience_survey_release_11-10-09.pdf.

[4]Ibid.

[5]"The Great Beyond: Is There Life After Death?" (survey, AARP, July 31, 2007).

8

RELATIONSHIPS FOR GROWN-UPS:

The Intricate Web

Marketers generally have an overly simplistic view of the Vibrant Woman's relationships, especially marketers who have been talking to her solely as a "mom" for the last twenty-five years of her life. While that single-relationship focus may work well for the woman with young children, it may also limit marketers' abilities to appreciate and speak to the much richer web of relationships through which a Vibrant Woman defines and makes her own life.

As we found in chapter 2, Vibrant Women represent the first generation of women whose connections—as well as variety of relationships—are expanding as they age. Nothing differentiates her further from her mother, whose social network shrank over time, than this degree of connectedness.[1] Even as marketers and the media perpetuate the outdated stereotypes that defined her mother, the Vibrant Woman is alternately finding herself socializing, working with, burdened by, influencing, reaching out to, and sometimes boldly leaving behind the people who make up the intricate web of her interpersonal connections. In other words, she is pioneering new territory for grown-up relationships at the intersection of longevity, technological, economic, and social trends.

While two-thirds of Vibrant Women remain in traditional marriages,[2] the appearance of a conventional life does not define or limit her universe of relationships. Rather, the Vibrant Woman's interpersonal terrain is packed with friends, business associates, community, and special interest connections...not to mention her beloved dog, horse, or cat. All this is above and beyond her inner circle of family relationships: a personal network of commitments, responsibilities, and interactions that is larger than she'd anticipated having at this or any stage of her life. Her parents are living longer, and many of her adult children have returned home—if they ever left at all. And with divorce rates high at multiple generational levels, many Vibrant Women are also dealing with the complexities of duplicate sets of ex-spouses, in-laws, step- and grandchildren.

RETOOLING FRIENDSHIPS

In fact, as consumed as she is with handling the emotional highs and lows of her extended family, one of the first surprises about her vibrant relationships is the drive and energy she has for making new friends. At 50+, Vibrant Women have shown themselves to be hungry for new and deeper connections with women at a similar age and stage in life. Nothing better illustrates how different Vibrant Women are from the women of previous generations. At 50+, regardless of whether or not she's post-menopausal, she doesn't feel "old" in any sense of the word. With thirty or more vital years ahead of her, the last thing she wants is to be marginalized. She knows that she both wants and needs to be connected with others, and when it comes to her relationships with others, she wants to get it right.

Among other things, getting it right means establishing richer and deeper relationships with "women like me." And in this regard, she is once again largely on her own. Her mother, centered in family and home, tended to make a handful of friends from her neighborhood

---

The lines are blurring between on- and off-line friendships.

---

or volunteer activities. Over time, as friends moved or passed away, she lost the potential to replace her friendships with her inner circle of women.

Vibrant Women, on the other hand, grew into adulthood in times of high mobility. Leaving home at an early age and exposed to multiple schools, travel, and work geographies, she was repeatedly put in the position of meeting new people. Unlike her mother, she developed the facility and desire for making new contacts over the years. Until the Internet gave her the means to stay connected, however, she tended to leave a trail of friendships in her wake as she progressed through

With thirty or more vital years ahead of her, the last thing she wants is to be marginalized.

lifestages and experiences. Superimposed upon lives already packed with her own family and work obligations, friendships were either more utilitarian in nature or more centered on her children than herself. In mid-life some women now recognize the price paid for this approach to friendships. She may have traded breadth for depth, a miscalculation now apparent as she commits herself to her maturing values. At the same time, she may be realizing that she has little in common with people who have been her "friends" primarily because their children went to the same schools or they lived in the same neighborhoods. Regardless, as she enters a new stage in life as mother of adult children, becomes a grandmother, finds herself suddenly single, and/or faces career and economic challenges, she discovers herself in the position of needing new or better support systems. As a result, a question we see frequently on VibrantNation.com is: "Where can I make new friends?"

Foremost among her resources is the Internet, where she can experience new connections with her peers. Whether she's finding old classmates on Facebook or using anonymous social networks, she is taking risks and reaching out to others, often at a more vulnerable level than in her "real" life. Increasingly, however, the lines are blurring between on- and off-line friendships, as women who meet on-line are taking their relationships into the nonvirtual world as well as enticing their friends on-line.

Given the important transitions a Vibrant Woman is going through, she wants peers who share her outlook at this stage of life. Many Vibrant Women report ending relationships with lifelong friends who fixate on the negative or seem more interested in closing than opening their minds as they age. And many Vibrant Women have known the pain of friend breakups as the "dumpee." The challenge of finding like-minded friends at her stage of life is not dissimilar from the challenge of dating for someone who suddenly finds herself single. Fortunately, Vibrant Women understand this challenge and are a lot more willing to help each other than when they were facing some of the same dilemmas as teenagers.

THE REFILLED NEST

Her desire for relationships with her peers notwithstanding, the Vibrant Woman's ability to hang out with girlfriends as much as she'd like is being postponed by the recession's impact on her family responsibilities. For the majority of Vibrant Women, the empty nest has filled back up again, as she finds herself running the equivalent of a multigenerational boarding house. In a VibrantNation.com survey almost two-thirds of our respondents reported that they have an adult child (or children) living at home. And almost half of those said that their adult child had brought one or more grandchildren with them. When you consider that another 13 percent reported that her own parents or in-laws are also living under her roof, and two-thirds have husbands at home, as well, it's no surprise that Vibrant Women are not finding as much free time as they'd like to spend with friends.[3]

What is most notable about this trend is that the Vibrant Woman is not seriously complaining about having to defer discretionary time in favor of extended time with family. In fact, 80 percent of the Vibrant Women we surveyed told us that, even if their adult children do stay at home longer than anticipated, this would fall somewhere on the scale between acceptable and terrific. Again, this represents a sea change from her mother's generation—women often hardened by the challenges of Depression and world war who gave birth young and expected her children to move on. Many Vibrant Women describe their mothers as "iron maidens," having held themselves back emotionally in order to build strong, independent children, following the parenting advice of their day.

Vibrant Women have been very different mothers to their children and will continue to aspire to establish much closer relationships with their offspring. As the first generation post-Women's Liberation, they waited longer to get their families started. By then, they were often immersed in their careers, alternately relishing their precious, quality time with their offspring and feeling guilty for the role they were playing in raising a generation of "latchkey kids." Many Vibrant Women continue to struggle with the tension between their desire to maintain or establish emotional

---

Many Vibrant Women describe their mothers as "iron maidens."

---

intimacy with their adult children versus setting them free to fend for themselves. At VibrantNation.com, we are also witnesses to the tension that women whose children have left home express regarding whether to savor or regret the big empty nest of a house she lives in without them. At the same time, there are many Vibrant Women who report the achievement of an aspirational milestone: establishing closer relationships with their own daughters and sons than they ever got to experience with their own mothers.

THE GRANDMOTHER PARADOX

The desire for emotional intimacy is heightened further when grandchildren enter the picture. Whether her grandchildren are under her own roof, nearby, or far away, the Vibrant Woman is a member of the first generation of women in history who are becoming grandmothers while fully engaged in the ongoing demands and opportunities of their own lives. As a result, she brings her now-familiar passion to this new role while at the same time doesn't want to be defined exclusively by it. This balance is not always easy for her children—or others—to understand and adds to the challenge of defining what successful grandparenting looks like.

However she works it out, you can be sure that she places a great deal of emotional energy on her relationship with her grandchildren. In support of her passion for deep involvement, she will stretch her resources to support them. This is likely to include covering such basics as helping out with housing and daily living costs, as well as paying for toys, clothing, and education. If she lives nearby, she can anticipate seeing her grandkids as often as she'd like and developing rich and meaningful relationships with them. When they live far apart, a good part of her discretionary income will be spent paying for transportation to and from each others' homes, with the intent

---

It is her desire to stay connected with her grandchildren that has been the primary catalyst for broadening her technological comfort zone.

---

on sharing as many holidays and special times together as possible. While distance poses a challenge, resourceful women are willing to go to extremes to help close the gap. In fact, it is her desire to stay connected with her grandchildren that has been the primary catalyst for broadening her technological comfort zone, as substantiated by the explosive growth of her presence on Facebook, Flickr, and Skype. And where there is the means, whether or not they live in close proximity to one another, there will be multigenerational vacations, reunions, and the like.

At the less rosy end of the spectrum, the Vibrant Woman's desire for involvement with the grandchildren may be thwarted

80 percent of Vibrant Woman continue to work outside the home.

by difficult relationships with adult children and their spouses or competition with in-laws. In fact, both chronic and acute disappointments can temper her desire to remain or become close to her children and grandchildren. But that disappointment cuts both ways. Among the key disappointments: adult children who expect mom to play the part of the traditional grandmother. At a time when the marginalized women of generations past would have been completely available to help out with raising the grandkids, 80 percent of Vibrant Women continue to work outside the home. Forget the images of grandma in the rocking chair with a baby on her lap. The Vibrant Woman loves her grandchildren and wants to spend quality time with them. But it will nevertheless be an item that will have to be scheduled into her already busy life.

"THE DAUGHTER TRAP"

While at its best, spending time with her grandchildren is available to her as an act of choice, managing her role as primary caregiver to aging parents and in-laws is one over which she has little control. Acknowledging the fact that so many Boomer women support both their adult children and their aging parents, many have called her the "Sandwich Generation." More recently, Boomer expert Laurel Kennedy referred to this phenomenon as "The Daughter Trap," the tacit understanding in the majority of families that it is the daughter who ends up assuming the family's elder-care responsibilities. As Kennedy, who experienced this firsthand, writes: "No one asks, everyone assumes, that a daughter will and can provide care." We've been acculturated to be nurturing, to take care

The caregiving tunnel is long, dark, and lonely.
But it inevitably comes to an end.

of people. It's traditional, a vestigial concept left over from when we lived on farms in extended families. But now, with 80 percent of women working outside the home, it's impractical and improbable that a woman can just drop everything and add elder care to her responsibilities. Yet somehow, we manage it, at great personal cost."[4]

Kennedy points out that the typical female caregiver forfeits funds, both in lost wages and out-of-pocket expenses, intended for her own financial future by providing care for another. But as great as the financial toll may be, the emotional investment is even higher. Some women find the time spent caregiving to be "a precious gift," achieving a level of intimacy and completion with their mothers and fathers that more than compensates for any of the sacrifices she makes. But the majority feels that they have been handed a heavier burden than any one person should ever be asked to handle on her own. Not only is she left alone to deal with the entire spectrum of emotional, physical, and logistical needs of the declining health of her parents, but she finds herself enmeshed in an intricate web of family dynamics that can surface resentments both old and new.

For most, the caregiving tunnel is long, dark, and lonely. But it inevitably comes to an end. Emerging back into the light of her own life, the Vibrant Woman often discovers that both her internal and external terrain has undergone dramatic shifts. Her relationships with her husband and siblings may be closer than ever before, but more often, the Vibrant Woman feels herself newly empowered to make fresh choices about how she intends to live her life. Her exposure to mortality can have a positive result: the determination to make her own life count, starting with a renewed emphasis on the quality and importance of her relationships.

But this is not entirely new to her. Every milestone at mid-life and beyond, from the initiation of menopause and children going off to college to the birth of grandchildren and adult offspring returning home, afford her with opportunities for personal growth. As we have seen throughout this book, whether viewing this woman through the lens of fashion and beauty, finances and well-being, and now her relationships with others, beneath it all, she is always in search of greater meaning.

EMPOWERED DECISIONS

As she crosses the threshold of 50 and beyond, she becomes increasingly and, in some cases, suddenly empowered to rethink the old and initiate the new. While she often struggles with her decisions, she believes she has earned the right to have people in her life who truly support her and who she is becoming. Siblings who are unwilling to pitch in, adult children who resist doing their share, and friends who she has simply outgrown may be put on notice that she is "breaking up" with them.

No one is exempt. In some cases, husbands of many years are shocked to discover that their wives would rather be on their own—or with someone else—than remain in long-term marriages that have outlived their usefulness. In fact, the demographic now most likely to initiate divorce, among all the cohorts, is none other than the woman 50+.[5] Feeling neglected, bored, or burdened by her spouse, she may have already stayed longer in the marriage than she'd wished "for the sake of the children" or plotted her escape timed to when the annuity or inheritance money is due, giving her the means to go out on her own. Whatever the reason, in the words of one Vibrant Woman: "The kids left the nest, and I walked right out behind."

Women who do leave their longtime marriages or find themselves suddenly single because a longtime husband did so, suddenly have questions they never thought they'd be asking their girlfriends. *How am I supposed to find someone to date? What should I wear? Am I crazy to consider getting married again?*

Although many women find themselves starting over, others use this more deliberate approach to strengthen their connections with their husbands. Many Vibrant Women enjoy marriages reinvigorated by a passionate and mature perspective.

Whether she's married or not, her desire for intimacy, love, and, for many, sex (the subject of the next chapter) is defying the stereotypes, growing stronger rather than diminishing over time.

IMPLICATIONS FOR MARKETERS

Marketers generally have an overly simplistic view of the Vibrant Woman's relationships. Many assume that the relationship their product or service addresses (whether caregiving, grandparenthood, or marriage) is the only concern on their target consumer's mind. But few Vibrant Women define themselves solely as "caregiver" or "grandmother." The failure to understand that for her any given relationship fits within a web of other relationships is a serious mistake.

This is especially true for marketers who have been talking to the Vibrant Woman solely as a "mom" for the last twenty-five years of her life. While that single-relationship focus may work well for the woman with young children, it may also limit marketers' abilities to appreciate and speak to the much richer web of relationships through which a Vibrant Woman defines and makes her own life.

What does this mean for marketers?

> To connect with women 50+, sell a product in terms of relationships, with your target Vibrant Woman consumer at the center.

> Vibrant Women are more than mothers, but they are still mothers. It's just that now she's a mother of 20 (or 30)-somethings instead of toddlers or teenagers.

> As important as relationships are, do not use a single relation to define her. While she may spend a lot of her time managing health care for her aging parents, for instance, she is unlikely to think of herself in the dead-end job description of "caregiver." She almost never uses this term to describe herself, so avoid it.

> Use relationships to sell to her. Consider using the world of "mommy bloggers" to encourage new mothers to promote products for their mothers.

> Make sure any spokesperson for your product looks like a person the Vibrant Woman would have (or want) as a friend.

> Since she is likely managing her own version of a "refilled nest," show her how your product or service will help her manage the boarding house that her briefly empty nest has now become.

> Finally, recognize that her dense web of relationships symbolizes her importance as the "Chief Purchasing Officer" for three or four generations of her own family. She is either working with her children or parents to identify—or herself buying— everything from laptop computers to health insurance to airplane tickets. The brands of suppliers who best support the relationships underlying her purchases will win more of her business.

The Voices of Vibrant Nation

ON STRUGGLING WITH CAREGIVING RESPONSIBILITIES

FROM A CONVERSATION ON VN

For many Vibrant Women, serving as primary caregiver to aging parents takes an emotional as well as financial and physical toll.

melodyann:

Letting go of the past with aging parents...

I am almost ashamed to write this, because the relationship between a child and her parent, especially her mother, is supposed to be sacred. My mother was a wonderful mom when I was young. She was perfect in every way, but as I grew up and "left the nest" things changed. She began to be more manipulative, dishonest, and controlling and needless to say we had our differences. What matters now is that she is 85 and in poor health and truly needs an advocate. While reading Amy Ferris's book Marrying George Clooney for the second time, so that I would be "up" on everything for the book club here at Vibrant Nation, I noticed a passage that I had missed somehow before—where Amy's mother who is in an assisted living situation, struggling with the beginnings of Alzhiemers, says to her I never wanted anyone to love you, I wanted them to love me! Amy says in her book that THIS is where the little girl in her and the adult Amy separate, and Amy goes in and lays on the bed next to her mother and hugs her.

This passage made me cry and cry because I realize the resentment I've been storing up and holding against my mother, even today, is the child in me, NOT the feelings of an adult. It is hard to let go of anger, very, vey hard, but there does reach a point where the anger turns on you and becomes toxic. I have struggled for the last several months because I have alternately hated and loved my mother, been kind and then abrupt and impatient with her, and it is only now, after reading that passage that I realize it is time to let go of the past. All she has really is me. And she truly needs an advocate at this stage in the game. She is very scared and insecure about her life. She has no control for the most part in what happens, and I can only imagine that she must feel terribly, terribly alone. We have only the now. Nothing else in our lives is guaranteed, and I know my actions (verbally short and impatient) have caused her pain. As Amy did in her book, it is time for me to let go of the little girl and grow into an adult and let go of what was then and grasp the importance of NOW. No matter how my mother handled things in the past, the only thing that matters is how I handle this now, and kindness, love, and compassion are the only tools when you're dealing with an aging parent.

I'm so appreciative for this book, and I hope every woman out there will find an opportunity to read and relate to the words as Ms. Ferris opens her heart and shares her innermost feelings with the reader. It's just nice to know we are not alone.

ON BREAKING UP WITH GIRLFRIENDS
FROM A CONVERSATION ON VN

While she often struggles with her decisions, the Vibrant Woman believes she has earned the right to have people in her life who truly support her and who she is becoming. This includes leaving behind even longtime friendships that she has outgrown.

lzwynn:

I had a girlfriend breakup this past summer of a very longtime friend. We had already had one breakup for a few years (she didn't like the fact that I was dating someone because it meant less time for her), but when she found out my husband died, she showed up on my porch one day and our friendship became, once again, very close. But then it became not fun anymore...again. I was trying to concentrate on being positive and a Christian woman, but I noticed how very negative she was. Her favorite past time was complaining—about her kids, money, whatever. It was really getting to me, and I was becoming seriously depressed. I kept asking myself "Why do you continue this friendship if every time you leave you are so down and in the dumps?" I thought I had to press on and endure because otherwise I would be alone with no friends. But one day as I was driving away I decided, for my own sake, that I just could not do this anymore. I wrote her a letter and explained that I loved her, but she had become so negative and I just could not handle it any longer. Of course, she was very angry and wrote me a nasty note. But, needless to say, we have not spoken since. Do I miss her? Yes. But it's better to be alone than live with all that negative, harsh, complaining, never-happy attitude stuff. That is just not healthy. Even as I write this, I am remembering some happy times when we would laugh so hard. But somewhere she lost herself and I almost lost mine. I live alone and work alone. So I do get lonely. BUT it's at least a healthy lonely.

I know we can't always keep ALL people who come into our lives. There are different seasons and people in those seasons. We just have to learn to love the good memories and be glad that we had the wisdom enough to get out of a harmful relationship.

Thank you, ladies, for writing your responses. I'm not glad you had breakups, too, but it is still somehow comforting to know that I'm not the only one who feels like this.

ON LIFE AFTER DIVORCE
FROM A CONVERSATION ON VN

Many Vibrant Women would rather be alone than to remain in a marriage that no longer serves her.

Metoo:

I have been through a divorce after twenty-seven years of marriage. Although I asked for the divorce, I would rather have seen us fix things, but he would have none of it, thwarted every attempt I made to get us help, etc, so I finally saved what was left of my life and divorced him. It was still devastating to be alone, deal with the kids' anger (they obviously didn't know the whole story), his anger, etc. It is now three years later, and I am in a MUCH better place with my life—and so is he, by the way. It takes time. Everyone is different, every situation is different, but things will get better. Talk out your feelings, write them out, seek counseling, and take excellent care of your health—healthy food, reasonable exercise, etc. You will heal.

silentnomore08:

I divorced after twenty-eight years of marriage. January 10 will be my second birthday of my new life as a single adult female over 50. I can assure you it is not the easiest thing I have ever done, but it is not the hardest either.

I tried to date about a year ago and realized that I was nowhere near ready to do that. I found myself in a nonphysical yet emotionally consuming relationship with a very good con-artist who uses women to survive. Thankfully two of us became friends and began to realize that he was lying to us and at least six other women at the same time. No wonder he was always so tired!!

Getting through that with my self-esteem and my financial situation intact taught me to be more careful, to trust my initial instincts (which I had not done in that situation), and to run things past my friends and counselor before getting in to deeply.

My advice is to be strong, be true to yourself, and believe that you are worthy of the best there is in a man, so don't settle for less than the best.

I have recently begun dating again, and I am very clear up front that I am not looking for a physically intimate encounter, but for a deeper soul relationship. It "clears out the weeds," as my grandmother used to say.

There is indeed a light at the end of the tunnel, and it is bright and beautiful, so keep on going.

ON RUNNING A MULTIGENERATIONAL BOARDINGHOUSE
FROM A CONVERSATION ON VN

Dealing with the empty nest is hard enough, but coping with adult kids, grandkids, and extended family who have moved back in again can be equally or more challenging.

NatalieC:

Empty nest and returning children is a complex situation. First there is the reality that you aren't who you were before your children left and neither are they. Each of your roles has changed. I remember one family talked to me about how they wanted their child to get that they are roommates now that he came back home. I don't think that is realistic. It is like saying that lovers can go back to being just friends. You aren't just roommates, you are family. The investment in it working out is deep because you are family. Biggest tip is continue to focus on yourself and don't fall back into the full-time parent role. Lower your *expectations that they will have family meals with you and be consistent in doing chores. They haven't lived on the planet as long as you have so they don't have the life learnings you do. State your needs and what is absolutely not negotiable, for example illegal drugs. Each family has their own values, so don't lose sight of them. Electric bills are usually consistent, so the returner/adult child can budget to pay for that bill. Text if they aren't coming home out of respect, so you don't have to worry if they are OK or not. Children don't always get that because you didn't know where they were when they weren't living at home, but you get to have that now as a nonnegotiable if it really matters to you. Renegotiate and do check-ins so resentment doesn't build. Truth is you don't resent them, but you resent yourself for not holding the line. Steady as you go. Enjoy the time as best you can, but for sure don't be treated in ways you wouldn't let anyone on the planet treat you, for example not raging and tantruming on you because their issues aren't handled. Let them know you don't let anyone treat you that way, and if it happens again, they need to find a way to course correct that, for example get out of the car and walk, call a friend, or do something that shifts the situation. It isn't easy being in a transition, so get support.*

ON EMOTIONAL INTIMACY WITH ADULT CHILDREN AND GRANDCHILDREN

BLOG BY CAROL ORSBORN, "INSIDE THE NATION"

Vibrant Women crave emotional intimacy with their grown children and grandchildren. But there can be a shadow side to the degree to which she is invested in the relationships.

Once a month, I gather with a group of us who are on track to being trained as spiritual directors. While we come from different ages and stages in life, when we dig deep enough, we find we have much in common.

Sometimes, what we address are the joyful themes. But at this weekend's gathering, our conversation turned somber, as we began sharing about various flavors of disappointment regarding our relationships to our children.

Of course, there are children who haven't fulfilled their potential, having difficulty establishing an adult life, doing drugs, and worse. But disappointment goes both ways. Adult children as well as their parents express sadness over having lost the closeness they had as a family growing up or never having been close in the first place. Some feel estranged from family members who live across the country. And then, there are those who do live in close proximity but who still find ways to disappoint one another.

Frankly, by the session's end, I was disturbed. What are we supposed to do with all this disappointment? I asked the group leader if we could speak privately for a few minutes. She readily agreed. We walked together from the meeting room to her private office. I immediately noticed that there were framed photos of her adult children and grandchildren lovingly scattered about. Surely, she would have the answer.

And in fact, she did. But it wasn't what I expected.

"You hope to find the direction you can turn in regards to your children that will not carry with it some degree of disappointment. But no matter how hard you try, it won't be enough. For beneath the push and pull of all the 'I wants,' 'I didn'ts,' and 'if onlys,' there is an existential disappointment that underlies all the others."

In a nutshell, here's what she told me. There are limitations to what anyone can do for anybody else, including one's beloved child. We cannot stop them from having pain or create for them a safe, easy world. In fact, we can't deliver on virtually any of the hopes and promises we made in our hearts for our children as we birthed, raised, and grappled with the challenge of releasing them to their destinies. The only hope and promise that we can hold onto, through all the disappointments of life, is that we love them no matter what.

I heard her, and it was a lot to take in. But it was getting late, and my guide indicated that it was time to go. As I lingered in front of one of the framed photos, she realized that I still wasn't sure.

We stood there quietly for a moment, and then she started to talk.

"This one..." she said pointing to the photo "is disappointed in me because I'm not as available to her to babysit as often as she'd like. This one..." she said pointing to another "needs more financial support than I'm able to give. I'd love to be able to send my grandchild to private school, and it hurts that I've had to say I can't." She sighed deeply.

"That is what we women do...our particular greatness. We endure."

I suddenly got what she was trying to tell me. The time had come for me to stop trying to address the problem of disappointment by attempting to defy the core limitations that are built in to the human condition. The only way to do this is to stop attempting to solve disappointments as if they were a problem and to willingly provide loving space for everything— including our disappointments—in our hearts.

It wasn't the answer I'd been hoping for, but as I noted the unshakeable look of peace on her face as she studied the photos, patted her own heart, and hugged me goodbye, strangely, it did not disappoint.

[1]Recall the research findings shared in chapter 2, which revealed that the average active thirty-day personal network for these Vibrant Women clocked in at a robust 46. For the most highly connected third of these women, that thirty-day network included an average of ninety-nine personal contacts a month. Moreover, over half of the women in the study confirmed that their active thirty-day personal networks had grown substantially in the past five years.

[2]The remaining one third is in the category "other," including divorced, widowed, single, and gay.

[3]"Full Nest Survey," VibrantNation.com, March 1, 2010.

[4]Q&A with Laurel Kennedy, *The Daughter Trap: Taking Care of Mom and Dad...and You* (New York: St. Martin's Press, 2010).

[5]Mary Brown and Carol Orsborn, *BOOM: Marketing to the Ultimate Power Consumer—The Baby-Boomer Woman* (New York: AMACOM, 2006).

[6]Amy Ferris, *Marrying George Clooney* (Berkeley, CA: Seal Press, 2009).

9

WHO'S YOUR GEORGE CLOONEY?

Love and the New Sexual Revolution

The Vibrant Woman's regained interest in sex and romantic relationships is not only busting stereotypes but catching her by surprise, as well. In fact, this 50+ woman is telling us that a new sexual revolution about what it means to be a sexual woman at mid-life is at hand. Adding to the headline-worthy nature of this new development, this is one sexual revolution that may or may not include men.

Topics where the mainstream marketing conversation is leaving out Vibrant Women are those where this woman's confidence about the future meets emotional or physical challenges particular to her lifestage and age. No one seems interested in talking about or helping her solve her particular weight loss challenges or manage her financial future in ways pertinent and meaningful to her. As a result, she gains special value from connecting with other women like her.

From observing the traffic and conversations that take place daily on VibrantNation.com, we know which one of these is the most sensitive topic of them all: love and sex. Almost all Vibrant Women want a meaningful relationship and a satisfying sex life. But obtaining these involves overcoming a host of hurdles. One of the key hurdles is a negative self-image centered around changes in her body. Those who had children, including the many who chose to begin or add to their families later in life, may still be experiencing the lingering effects of childbirth. Moms and grandmothers, as well as women who have never had children, encounter the impact of menopause on their libido and sex organs. And all women 50+ also face the silence that shrouds questions about what makes for appropriate sexual desire and fulfillment at their age and stage in life.

Her regained interest in the topic of sex and romantic relationships is consistent with the 50+ woman's often newfound focus on fitness, independence, and the accelerated progress toward self-actualization that we described in chapter 3. In this case, however, her passion is not only busting stereotypes but catching her by surprise, as well. In fact, this 50+ woman is telling us that a new sexual revolution about what it means to be a sexual woman at mid-life is at hand. Adding to the headline-worthy nature of this new development, this is one sexual revolution that may or may not include men.

This is not to say that the Vibrant Woman isn't married—perhaps happily so. Previously, we reported that two-thirds of them have spouses, including longtime married couples whose love and

---

All women 50+ face the silence that shrouds questions about what makes for appropriate sexual desire and fulfillment at their age.

---

sexual relations with their husbands have grown only stronger over the years. Writes Vibrant Nation member DallasLady: "There is nothing more blissful than an excellent marriage with a wonderful man who loves you unconditionally. I have that man. And I wouldn't trade my life for ANYTHING. I don't care if he snores. I don't care if his jokes are corny. Because he has lived up to every single one of those vows."

But our recent surveys of women 50+, coupled with divorce statistics, indicate that this happy convergence of traditional marriage and sexuality tends to be the exception, rather than the rule.[1]

TURNING THE BIOLOGICAL CLOCK BACK

All the trends we addressed previously, from economic independence and improved physical fitness to a desire for relationships that matter, play a role in this area of her life. Physically fit, the Vibrant Woman's body is more attuned to the potential for ongoing sexual vitality than the postmenopausal women of generations past. Hormonal replacement therapy can turn back the clock on her sexual attributes, desires, and abilities. Many women undertake the risks hormone therapy may pose just to gain the sexual pleasure it can provide.[2] At the same time, the financially self-sufficient empty-nester has fewer reasons than when she had younger children in her home to remain in an unfulfilling marriage. As in other areas, this is a woman who is frequently defying the stereotypes, in this case of a gradual decline into the passivity of an asexual old age. In many cases, she is a woman who believes she is free from the constraints of the past, and yet ready to reach her peak in many areas of her life, including her sexuality. But more often than not, all indications are that she remains unsure as to whether this kind of satisfaction is genuinely possible for her.

Beneath all the trends, there is one event that has been most influential, laying the groundwork for successive sexual revolutions: the continuing impact of the birth control pill. Leading-edge

---

By postponing or avoiding child-rearing, they could devote their considerable energy to advancing careers and developing skills, interests, and abilities.

Boomer women were the first cohort to come of age in the era of "the Pill," their younger sisters following closely behind. It was the Pill, above all, that forged the connection between women's liberation and sexual freedom. For the first time in history, women of childbearing age could dependably choose when or if to bear children. By postponing or avoiding child-rearing, they could instead devote their considerable energy to advancing careers and developing skills, interests, and abilities. Simultaneously, they could engage in sexual activity divorced from concerns as to whether one's partner(s) would make a suitable father or mate.

THE PILL: A TWO-EDGED SWORD

While the economic benefits that came about as the result of the Pill are obvious, sexual liberation had its shadow side, as well. On the upside, women were presented with the opportunity to explore and fulfill their sexuality. On the downside, it brought new risks, like the rise in divorce and sexually transmitted diseases, including HIV/AIDS, all of which added layers of complexity, ambivalence, and outright danger to fulfilling that potential.

Then, too, the idea that she was free to choose whether and when to become a mother—and that by exercising that choice she would make a more intentional life than her mother's—often turned out to be false. First, the psycho-biological urge to have children often trumped more rational decision making. Second, at the exact same time that she gained her sexual independence, our culture began pounding at her with the message that she could be more liberated than her mother by "having it all."

Women made a valiant attempt to achieve that goal, often putting their own personal needs at the bottom of the list as they drew upon reserves of energy to manage their own careers, shuttle their children to an ever-longer list of achievement-oriented activities, and

> Our culture began pounding at her with the message that she could be more liberated than her mother by "having it all."

maintain a house and dinner table to which even a liberated husband contributed far less than she. In the face of conflicting demands, one of the first personal needs this multitasking woman often dropped was sex: ironic, given that the freedom to have sex without risk of more children was one of the Pill's great promises. As one of our Vibrant Nation members, Lynnette, wrote: "I was exhausted for twenty years."

REAWAKENING TO THE PROMISE

For the postmenopausal woman, the freedoms the Pill promised may have returned,and not too late for her to enjoy them. As the Vibrant Woman increasingly gains control over her own time and desires, she is reawakening to the promise of sexual liberation that was to be her generational birthright. At the same time, in this moment of transition, it sometimes appears that there is a big discrepancy among Vibrant Women. On one side of the divide, there are women 50+ who enthusiastically embrace a new life of sex and dating. Some, like Samantha Jones, the character played by Kim Cattrall (now 54) in *Sex and the City*, inspired by the "Cougar" phenomenon, now think, talk about, and act on their sexual urges with relish. For others on the lustier side of the divide, maturity, self-acceptance, and newfound time and space (the empty nest, after all, has its benefits) have allowed them to explore and enjoy a new kind of sexual pleasure (whether partnered or alone) that is slower, more intimate, and more intense. Both of these categories of women on this side of the divide say that sex after 50 is better.

On the other side of the divide, there are women who think of sex primarily as a problem. Libidos that pregnancy put on ice can prove challenging to kick back into gear. In addition, sometimes the libido is strong, but the body won't cooperate; for many women 50+, intercourse has become a painful activity. While some women say they accept a life without sexual pleasure, most refuse to adopt the "grin and bear it" attitude of sexual resignation many of their mothers accepted at or before mid-life. Empowered by the anonymity of the Internet, whether to order products or talk with peers, women in sexless marriages who haven't had an orgasm in years, many of whom have been unconsciously influenced by the stereotypes of asexualized older women, are finding the courage to raise issues (and share techniques) with one another.

THE "SEX AND THE SEASONED WOMAN" CONTROVERSY

The phenomenon of aging women shaking off sexual stereotypes is so new that even when Gail Sheehy published her taboo-challenging book titled *Sex and the Seasoned Woman,* controversy erupted.[3] Not only did men and younger women openly express disgust at the notion of older women having sex, but women 50+ also chimed in with strong, divergent opinions.

According to Sheehy: "On one side are women who take comfort in Old Think–that older women are doomed to invisibility, discarded by husbands looking for rejuvenation with fecund females carrying fresh eggs, and shunted aside in the corporate world in favor of coltish newbees. These women take consolation in seeing the cards as stacked against them and claiming permission to let themselves go, gather together, maybe drink a little too much, and swap their sour stories. On the other side are women like those I've interviewed all over the country–400 of them. They belong to a new universe of lusty, liberated women who were thrilled to be asked about their love and sex lives. Nobody ever asked before!"[4]

Since 2006, many more millions of Vibrant Women have entered, and possibly tipped the scales, toward what Sheehy calls a "new universe" of women for whom lust is an open, and not an

---

"They belong to a new universe of lusty, liberated women who were thrilled to be asked about their love and sex lives. Nobody ever asked before!"

---

embarrassing, condition of life. While many conversation topics enjoy robust activity at VibrantNation.com—from parenting adult children and financial advice to beauty products and exercise tips— our #1 searched topic is "love & sex."

In the words of Vibrant Nation member Kath56ryn: "Mid-life women tend to have more time to nurture themselves instead of being everyone else's caretaker. When you look at it that way, it begins to make sense that you would be more awake and aware now than you were at 30." Vibrant Women across the board are consulting sex counselors, physicians, books, and each other regarding both relationship and sexual issues. *Which lubricant should I use? Can I have sex on a first date? Can anybody tell me where my G Spot is? Have you tried on-line dating?* It is both the magnitude and forthrightness of this cohort's stereotype-defying interest in sexuality that constitutes the core of the sexual revolution at hand, a movement that is just now stirring to life.

THE VIBRANT NATION SEX SURVEY

While they may be overturning the status quo, Vibrant Women have not arrived en masse on the shores of sexual fulfillment—at least not within the context of their current relationship. In our most recent VibrantNation.com survey regarding sexual attitudes, over one-third report that their sex lives are "nonexistent" and wish it weren't so. When added to other responses, we identified a solid majority (some 60 percent) of respondents who are less than satisfied with their sex lives today. Many, even in otherwise happy marriages, often report that they would like a more vibrant sex life.

But that's not the end of the story, because at the same time, eight out of ten Vibrant Women feel empowered to find their own sources of pleasure and explore alternatives to fulfill their sexual needs. Some who are no longer married are dating on-line, others are experimenting with same-sex relations, and the vast majority— both married and single—are "taking matters into our own hands" with masturbation and sex toys. In fact, a stereotype-busting 80 percent of all respondents report that they masturbate, and 66

percent noted that they either own sex toy(s) such as a vibrator and/
or dildo or are definitely interested in obtaining one.[5]

On-line dialogue paints an even more complete and robust picture.
For instance, in a highly trafficked conversation regarding sex toys,
VibrantNation.com member and sexual expert Joan Price offers an
endorsement of the Hitachi Magic Wand: "It ranks right up there with
the automobile and the iPod as one of technology's greatest inventions."
Elsewhere on the site, in a conversation regarding age and gender-
appropriate erotic literature, Price recommends a particular memoir
by 58-year-old Rae Padilla Francoeur about her affair with a 67-year-
old.[6] Per Price's review, the book is "hot, very hot, explosively hot. Rae
describes the passionate details—how he touches and controls her
body, how her passions smolder, build, and erupt." Price compliments
the author for finding a way to utilize language the women of her
generation would be more comfortable with (such as penis and vagina)
than the vulgar euphemisms or edgier words that have typified erotic
literature meant to appeal to younger or male readers.

SEX AND ROMANCE—OR NOT

Just as the Pill introduced the potential for sex without serious
commitment in the 1960s, so does life after menopause open up the
potential for sex without romance for women 50+. In the words of
one VibrantNation.com member: "Myth #6: Older women must have
romance to have sex. *False, though many do desire connection. Most
women tend to like being wined and dined. But, many women over
50 prefer easy encounters and/or friends with benefits. They like
their independence and they like sex. They prefer no muss, no fuss.*"
The comment, while embraced by many members, also engendered
lively communication, with a number of women confessing that
even though they know better, they'd still like a man in their lives—
preferably with a ring attached.

"I met my life-partner seventeen months after my husband's death...and, frankly, no one was more surprised than I."

Married or not, they also have no problem closing the gap between present reality and aspirations with healthy doses of fantasizing. VibrantNation.com member Amy Ferris, author of *Marrying George Clooney*, tapped a nerve with her best-selling memoir, subtitled *Confessions from a Midlife Crisis*.[7] Kept awake nights by hot flashes, Amy in her book portrays herself as ricocheting back and forth between fantasizing about marrying George Clooney, googling old boyfriends, and researching obscure and fatal diseases on the Web. While Ferris happens to be married, women who are divorced, widowed, and even gay identified with her crush on Clooney and responded to the on-line question "Who's your George Clooney?" with crushes of their own.

While many are content to keep their crushes virtual, others report that they'd desire nothing more than a passionate love affair and/or a committed relationship, but not necessarily with a man. Writes Vibrant Nation member Shifting energy: "I was married to a man for twenty-five years. I did not sit down and say to myself, 'Self, let's try a woman this time.' I simply, amazingly, wonderfully, fell in love with the most amazing human, who just happened to be a woman." And Maat45 chimes in: "I met my life-partner seventeen months after my husband's death...and, frankly, no one was more surprised than I."

As a generation of women known for breaking new ground and finding their own answers, we know that Boomer women remain both vibrant and active in all aspects of their lives. They are proactively defying the notion that women who pass the threshold of menopause not only become invisible, but asexual. Despite this final and most persistent of all stereotypes, it should by now be no surprise to anybody that when it comes to sexuality, she would bring the same passion and problem-solving resourcefulness to her yearnings, issues, and opportunities that she has applied to all aspects of her life. Some Vibrant Women might blush, but they won't deny the compliment offered by one of their own, author Suzanne Braun Levine, when she refers to these passionate, fully-alive women as "Ripe Juicy Tomatoes."[8]

IMPLICATIONS FOR MARKETERS

As a matter of marketing in this category, whether it involves dating services, medication, or sex toys, our advice remains consistent:

> **Tell the Vibrant Woman that you know she can enjoy the fullest life possible, including the sexual and romantic life she deserves.** Then provide her with solutions for her issues. For example, Vibrant Women are quick to surface resentment at Big Pharma for developing and marketing Viagra (and other products focused on erectile dysfunction) long before it developed a product that would enhance sexual pleasure for women. But because the reasons for sexual dissatisfaction among 50+ are not uniform (like erectile dysfunction is for men), it seems unlikely to find a one-pill solution. Pharmaceutical companies should be paying attention to the diverse sources of sexual dissatisfaction among women in devising solutions that will address the needs and desires of real women 50+.

> **While again, many Vibrant Women readily admit to having issues regarding love and sex, opportunities for marketers abound.** The last decade has seen sexual products like lubricant become far more commonly available; the average

drugstore now offers dozens of varieties of KY, Astroglide, and other brands. We have not seen much evidence that manufacturers or retailers of these products appreciate the important market they have in Vibrant Women. In a recent VibrantNation.com survey, 22 percent of women reported that intercourse is painful for them and yet 75 percent don't have a favorite lubricant.[9] There is a great untapped opportunity for one (or more brands) to become the favored (and most recommended) brand of lubricant for postmenopausal women.

> **Vibrant Women call upon their many resources to establish new, more sexually complete relationships than at any time in their last twenty-five to thirty years.** The woman 50+ is not just daydreaming. She's acting on her desires. This may help account for the fact that VibrantNation.com abounds with stories of relationships that began on eharmony or match.com. Eharmony focuses on the emotional nature of matchmaking–not that it doesn't lead quickly to physical connections as well. VibrantNation. com blogger and artist Sarah Carter describes sending a portrait of herself naked (from the rear) to the man she met on-line. While others sites like Match.com and Jdate also reach a large segment of Boomers, every business built on relationships should assume that part of their market will be women 50+ either unsure how to find those relationships elsewhere or interested in exploring entirely new adventures (like lesbian sex).

> **In general, when discussing sex, use explicit but non-crude terms over euphemisms.**

> **Take advantage of this window of opportunity to develop and market the product of choice.** For instance, two out of three Vibrant Women report that they either own a sex toy/vibrator or are interested in getting one, but almost none can identify a brand name they respect in the category. Therefore, there

are clear opportunities to become the product of choice. Smart marketers and retailers will look for better ways to cater to this important yet frequently overlooked Boomer demographic.

> **Go straight to the experts.** Young marketers may always have a hard time imagining the sex lives of women the age of their mothers. For that reason, companies should consider other ways to overcome this psychological obstacle. First, engage Vibrant Women directly in developing ideas for the products and services as well as the messages they seek in this area. Second, consider hiring Vibrant Women as marketers for products whose application they themselves can appreciate.

The Voices of Vibrant Nation

ON SEXUAL MYTHS ABOUT WOMEN OVER 50
BLOG BY DR. DORREE LYNN, "FIFTY AND FURTHERMORE"

Many women would welcome a committed relationship with a man, but others prefer "no muss, no fuss."

1. Myth #1: Older women are lousy lovers.

False. For centuries, in many countries, it was expected that a young man would be initiated into the world of sexual pleasures by an older woman. Ladies, break the myths and reveal the lies. One way to do this is to hold your head up high and believe in yourself. You have history and experience on your side. Use it. You've lived long enough to have earned your stature.

2. Myth #2: Older women don't want sex as much as older men do.

False. Women just want more talk along with sex. Women love foreplay and feeling desired. If your partner doesn't "get it" suggest a date night away from the bedroom and gently talk to him (or her) about what you want. Communication is the key.

3. Myth #3: Older women's sex drive diminishes more quickly than older men's.

False. It's just more complex. Remember sex is more than penetration. Many women can have multiple orgasms forever. But, cuddling, touching, and sharing are all part of sex. If hormone help is needed, there are many traditional and alternative aids. And exercise always helps.

4. Myth #4: Older women don't want oral sex.

False. Some do, but some don't. If oral sex has never been your thing, you may not want it. On the other hand, you may love it. Or, you may want to try it and find out. Sexual preferences are as varied as we are.

5. Myth #5: Older women don't fantasize.

False. Many have active fantasy lives. An added hint: if you are fantasizing about your shopping list while making love, try something or someone sexier. Some studies show that women are turned on by eyes, faces, and butts. Also many women fantasize about strangers and movie stars. Fantasies are normal and natural ways the mind works.

6. Myth #6: Older women must have romance to have sex.

False, though many do desire connection. Most women tend to like being wined and dined. But, many women over 50 prefer easy encounters and/or friends with benefits. They like their independence and they like sex. They prefer no muss, no fuss.

7. Myth #7: Older women lose their vaginal sensitivity.

False. It depends on the woman. While for many women, hormone changes can cause painful vaginal dryness, this is not always the case. In addition to suggestions listed in #3, remember use it or lose it is the key. Vibrators are perfectly acceptable health aids.

ON HAPPY SEX FOR ONE
FROM A CONVERSATION ON VN

Vibrant Women may be less than satisfied with their sex lives—but are more than willing to take matters into their own hands.

lovesalot:

After reading several posts from women aching for sensual pleasure, I just want to suggest a simple way to ecstasy: turn off the phone, lock the door, and get under a good warm shower. Take the head off the shower and control the flow with your thumb. Play with the flow along the outer edges of your Cave of Paradise. Experiment with your breathing, tensing your muscles deep inside (pull them up), moving your hips, and also pushing down on the balls of your feet, all the while using the stream of water to awaken your amazing, incredible femaleness. Be patient, be adventurous, and from now on you never have to feel alone and "left out" of the fun! This can be profoundly satisfying and joyful for women in and out of all kinds of relationships.

Sharon:

Water sports are my favorite! The showerhead in our cabin in the mountains is one of the things I miss most when we are not there. It has three speeds certain to bring me to the garden of eden: "low," "medium," and "who needs a man."

Tamara:

This sounds like a bathroom accident just waiting to happen...you know, most tragedies happen in the bathroom. Just sayin...

New-name:

My showerhead doesn't come off the wall (I'll work on changing that). I get lonely and depressed being alone with the buzzing piece of plastic.

Sunblossom:

That's why I have a man....(well, one of the reasons any way).

New-name:

I have one, but sex is gone, and it was very one-sided when it was there. Imagine the most one-sided sex you can, and that was us. I never had an orgasm (is that OK to say here? TMI?). I explained more about this within someone's post called "married or single." I'm both.

Sunblossom:

Not TMI—as far as I'm concerned no taboo subjects here on VN! I have found I just have to approach sex a little differently with an older man.....but I want my "O" and doggone it as long as he is around and able, I'm going to get it—one way or another!(Although I will qualify that I am pretty much open to trying anything new, shower head is sadly affixed firmly to the wall also!).

Old tom boy:

It took my friend, Steve Showerhead, to teach me what the big O was all about. I was married for twenty-seven years to a less than great lover. It has kept me satisfied for many a year and not silly enough to settle for another fool just for sex. I would also say don't knock it til you try it. And yes, I have a Water Pik with multiple settings. I think a man in the shower with me might make it more interesting, but I'm not sure about better. They like to have it their way, and I always get it my way.

steelmagnolia:

A handheld shower can be a woman's best friend :) I admit it, my handheld shower gives me the best orgasms. I am going to miss that handheld shower; it stays with the house and STBXH (soon to be ex

husband), and I am going to miss him, the shower head, not the husband! The handheld shower that I have in my apartment would do the trick, except the water pressure is bad. I have complained to management, but they haven't been able to fix it,because pressure is fine everywhere else :(
Oh, well, I won't be in this particular apartment forever.
teritwo:

I am off to Home Depot to replace my shower head to a handheld one.

ON RULES FOR A FIRST DATE KISS?
FROM A CONVERSATION ON VN

Women who thought they'd be "through" with sex by 50, are finding themselves on new terrain without a road map. Seeking the shelter of anonymity, they can turn to one another for advice on-line.

SandyHeart:

What kind if any should you do on first date? Does your age make a difference? What kind of impression does it give?
Dallas Lady:

We are 50 something—the rules are out the window. Kiss the man if you are attracted to him already. Passionately ~!

For myself, I didn't go into full make-out session though. And as far as anything else....well, I didn't go there either on a first date (or a second!)

I refuse to discuss the third one on the Internet though!
Petitetiger:

Ditto. And I will add that life is short, and it's time to start enjoying it.
Kath56ryn:

If your date has gone well, and you are pleased to have met and spent time with him, a gentle good-bye kiss on the cheek or lips is not out of order. You want to leave him looking forward to more. If you are just getting to know one another, you don't want to introduce the variable of too much sensuality; that will obscure the more important factors. Aren't regrets usually about moving too quickly, rather than too slowly? It's very challenging to back up in the physical realm and return to an earlier level. Take it slowly and let things develop at an unhurried pace. The anticipation is sweet, and in addition you get to see what your date does with your boundaries.

KLE:

If you feel like kissing on the first date, go for it. I've had only one experience since my divorce, and my date kissed me good-night on the second date. I was ready. After that date we were involved with more intense kissing. I really liked all of that, but he wasn't the keeper type, so I quit seeing him. Did not want to get emotionally involved with someone who I knew would not be good for me down the road.

ON HAVING AN AFFAIR
FROM A CONVERSATION ON VN

Women at 50+ are on uncharted territory regarding how to fulfill their sexual needs. Turning to one another under the cover of on-line anonymity is allowing them to make better, informed decisions.

EllenP:

Can I keep my marriage while having an affair?

I'm happy in my marriage, except for the sex. I love my husband, but after twenty-eight years of marriage, I'm just not attracted to him sexually anymore, and he seems to have given up. I'm thinking of taking a friend up on his offer to "help me out," but I wonder if the French are right in their attitudes. Is it really possible to sustain a happy marriage while having an affair?

Amy:

I fear that our U.S. society doesn't agree with the French, Japanese, or any of the other cultures that turn their heads the other way while married folk have affairs. The most recent scandal that occurred with the Republican Senator should prove this to you. It just isn't accepted as easily as the movies and media wants us to think. The only way that I can see that this would work is IF your husband agreed to your doing this. Some partners will if they are open enough, but I haven't met a man yet that easily shares his woman with another man without a fight...for her or the relationship. I have a forum filled with men who are heartbroken over the fact that their wives are having affairs...leaving the marriage and children behind because they are not happy in the bedroom.

My question to you would be: Why aren't you attracted to him sexually anymore? What has he exactly given up on—having sex, you, the marriage, or trying to make you happy?

WoodsFTL:

A marriage is more than sex—sex is just one part. Do you still love your husband? Do you have fun together? Do you have common interests? Are you willing to throw all that away just for sex?

But to the point of your question—regardless of what other cultures are doing, could you live with the guilt?

My beliefs are that marriage is between one man and one woman till death do us part (I've been happily married for thirty-five years thank you). "Stepping out" on my husband, whether for sex or for friendly socialization or emotional bonding, would be cheating. Period. Can you live with yourself while you cheat?

Please discuss the situation with a trusted counselor (why are you discussing it with this "friend" who has offered to "help you out"?). As Amy said, What is it about your husband that is no longer attractive? Think about what attracted you at the beginning—make a list, think of events and places.

Hautblossom:

I know that this is a tough one, and I sympathize. I've been through some similar thoughts. I love my husband, and I'm happily married, but until three weeks ago, we hadn't had sex in over four years. I thought a lot about finding sex somewhere else. But as I talked it through with my counselor (over many sessions), I came to realize that in the end, I would be dishonoring myself to betray my husband in that way. It's not a matter of what is objectively "right"; it's a matter of how I was raised and what my core beliefs about honor are.

I think people sometimes underestimate the importance of sex as part of marriage. It's not really fair to characterize it as "just sex." It's a precious expression of intimacy. It's a place where you expose yourself to another person absolutely and trust that you will be loved and supported in your nakedness (emotional even more than physical). And, as important, it's a place where you accept and cherish and love your husband's nakedness. That intimacy and mutual trust is a treasure, and it spills over into the rest of your marriage.

ON A BETTER TERM FOR "BOYFRIEND"
FROM A CONVERSATION ON VN

The changing nature of sexual relationships calls for a new vocabulary. Vibrant Women are making it up as they go.

Ladysmith:

I met my boyfriend (if someone can give me a better word—I am 52 and he's 60—we live together, but are not married) on-line too. It has been great. I was married unhappily for twenty years, and this time around this relationship works. I work at it, and it is so much fun. It can work.

Old tom boy:

Don't you hate that term at our age. I think we need to make a concerted effort to start a new term. I sometimes use the "man in my life." Whoever thought we would be having boyfriends at this age, unless you are lucky enough to be a first-rate cougar.

Ladysmith:

I have also used that term "the man in my life," sometimes I just say "my new man." It's funny how when an older man can refer to his "girlfriend" it doesn't seem so odd!!

Sunblossom:

I never know what to call him. After seven years, he sure seems like a husband. I suppose partner works, but it would seem awkward to say, "I'd like you to meet my partner, Dave...." It sounds like we just made a business deal or something. In that last job interview I had, the guy who interviewed me referred to himself as his girlfriend's partner in business and partner in life.

Mostly I just use his name and do not define our relationship in the introduction. Hopefully they'll figure it out when I can't keep my hands off him.

I am always introduced as "my friend, Kathy," which really doesn't cover at all what I am to him. It always seems so "less than" a wife, and that is truly what I am, even without the paperwork.

Companion makes me seem like a Golden Retriever...and old!

So, what I said just this morning when I was introduced to someone is "Hi, I am Kathy. Dave's girl and partner in life." If he doesn't like that, he can correct me, and I'm doomed to being his "friend" unless we come up with another term.

GloJean:

Yes, I agree..."boyfriend" is out! The term implies we are trying to be teenagers again, which in a way is offensive to our now mature and respectful position in life. We could say "fiancé," but this is really not true, because we are not getting married. So what do we call a committed relationship where we are living together? Sorry, there doesn't seem to exist one in OUR society, anyway. Perhaps since we are all becoming able to live longer, many single seniors are adopting the living together happily without the strings attached. Does this mean we are less devoted to our partners, NO. And maybe if many more of us pursue this life it will become socially acceptable.

In the meantime, I just say, "This is my companion, _____."

dillin257:

For the last ten years, I have been saying "my partner, Dennis." I couldn't say husband or boyfriend, I'm not into "lover," and I guess I wanted people to know my "partner" was a man. IF his name had been Chris or Sam etc., I'd have to go to a second level of explanation. I'm not against any other kind of relationships, but I just wanted it known which one I was in. So, part of getting married tomorrow resolves this problem. Since I'm not changing my name and am sticking with my birth name, I'll still get called Mrs. "Birthname" at the grocery store, but that's OK. I agree we need a new word, something short. "My ex" seemed natural, so maybe "my next" or hmmmm.....have to think about it.

P.S., After Dennis and I living together for three years, the people across the street asked me if he was my brother. Seemed weird.

ON OVERCOMING THE STEREOTYPES

BLOG BY JOAN PRICE, "BETTER THAN I EVER EXPECTED"

Vibrant Women are waking up from the old stereotypes of being invisible and asexualized at mid-life and beyond...but at different rates.

Do you think aging has made you less attractive? Do you have difficulty seeing yourself or your partner as sexy and desirable?

Then it's time to challenge your own as well as society's perception that only young bodies and unlined faces are sexy and beautiful. We need to accept—no, celebrate!—our wrinkles and rejoice in all the pleasure these bodies can still give us.

Let's join together and practice rejecting society's youth-oriented view of beauty, keeping ourselves fit so that we feel happy with our bodies, and keeping a loud, buoyant sense of humor!

I loved my 71-year-old husband Robert's face and body. I looked into his vibrant blue eyes, and I saw the young man as well as the older man. The older man was no less sexy than the younger man must have been (I didn't know him then). In fact, he was more sexy, because he had learned how to live joyfully and love completely in ways that a young man can't know until he has lived a full life.

I look in the mirror, where new wrinkles seem to appear weekly. I try to walk my own talk, accepting my own face as I accepted Robert's, telling myself these wrinkles are badges of living, laughing, and loving. I tell myself, this is the youngest I'll ever be from now on!

I asked my 103-year-old great aunt what it felt like to be more than a hundred. She said, "I'm the same person I always was."

So are we. Rather than trying to deny our aging—which is futile anyway—let's celebrate it.

---

[1] Recall that the demographic most likely to initiate divorce is women 50+.

[2] Of course, as we wrote in chapter 7, it is both a shame and a missed opportunity that pharmaceutical companies, physicians, and the health-care establishment as a whole don't pay as much attention to addressing her unique medical issues without exposing her to harmful side effects as they do to male medical issues.

[3] Gail Sheehy, *Sex and the Seasoned Woman* (New York: Ballantine Books, 2006).

[4] Gail Sheehy, "Who's Afraid of the Seasoned Woman," *Huffington Post*, February 2006.

[5] "Sex Survey," VibrantNation.com, June 22, 2010, http://www.vibrantnation.com/assets/3132/Vibrant_Nation_sex_survey3.pdf.

[6] Rae Padilla Francoeur, *Free Fall: A Late-in-Life Love Affair* (Berkeley, CA: Seal Press, 2010).

[7] Amy Ferris, *Marrying George Clooney: Confessions from a Midlife Crisis* (Berkeley, CA: Seal Press, 2009).

[8] Susan Swartz, *The Juicy Tomatoes Guide to Ripe Living after 50* (Oakland, CA: New Harbinger Publications, Inc., 2006).

[9] "Sex Survey," VibrantNation.com, June 22, 2010.

10

THE GOOD LIFE...

Vibrant Nation-Style

The real key to engaging the Vibrant Woman requires a deeper appreciation of her underlying needs: she is vital, dynamic, sometimes surprisingly insecure, but always aspiring not only to live the good life, but something even more compelling: her own life.

The Vibrant Woman has broken new ground as she matured into each previous decade and will do so again in the 2010s. While we've detailed the challenges brought on by both the recession and the aging process, the Vibrant Woman is now seeing her lifelong progress reflected everywhere from sales charts to the silver screen. Where earlier decades reflected her role in the workplace and her approach to motherhood, this decade will reflect the dramatic growth in population and spending power among women 50+.

This is the era in which the Boomer woman shocked the music industry by rocketing sales of Susan Boyle's album to record-breaking levels. Women 50+ create and move entire markets in consumer goods, ranging from antiaging cosmetics to hybrid automobiles. This Vibrant Woman has chocked up significant air miles and was the fastest growing demographic both on Facebook and in health club memberships.

And as we noted earlier, this was also the era in which a Vibrant Woman made history by capturing the first Oscar for best picture of the year (*Hurt Locker*), and film director Nancy Meyers and star Meryl Streep, also 50+, brought a new narrative for Vibrant Women to theaters around the world. In their movie *It's Complicated* Streep's role was the 60+ Jane, a Vibrant Woman pursued and seduced by both her ex-husband and the architect for the addition she planned for her home. The film delivered the persuasive message that women at mid-life and beyond can be sexy, vital, prosperous, and the center of attention. But as important as her romantic relationships are in this film, there is another, even more central love interest worth noting: Meyer's vision of "the good life," a lifestyle, sensibility, and taste level that are clearly aspirational, but speak volumes about what many Vibrant Women value, admire, and appreciate.

As a successful retailer, Jane can afford not only a new dream kitchen in her home but also the addition of a second-floor bedroom with a panoramic view right from her bed. She travels for family events, and she gardens. There is nothing gaudy or gauche about her lifestyle. Neither, however, is there any hint of embarrassment about spending money for what she wants. From the fashionable overstuffed furniture in her living room to the state-of-the art pots and pans, you sense that she is willing to pay for quality, but

---

This Vibrant Woman has chocked up significant air miles and was the fastest growing demographic both on Facebook and in health club memberships.

---

uninterested in buying things she doesn't need, things that won't last, or things meant primarily to impress.

It is quality of relationships, rather than the lure of status, that drives her decisions, like those of most Vibrant Women. Whether cooking a potluck meal with friends or sipping a martini at a classy New York bar, her focus has shifted to experience, rejuvenation, and personal growth. In fact, aside from the cost of Jane's remodel and a trip to New York for her son's graduation from college, the largest single indulgence portrayed in the film is an emergency session with her psychologist. The core of his advice: the good life, above all, is not one without risks. The greatest risk of all: ignoring the dictates of her heart.

Our insider's study of Vibrant Women concludes with a whirlwind tour through the landscape of her lifestyle: specifically, how she engages with and spends her money in a variety of key consumer categories. Alternately driven, curious, and inspired in her choices, this woman at 50+ has become the quintessential grown-up. While reviewing our detailed insights into her motivations as a shopper, remember that the real key to engaging the Vibrant Woman requires a deeper appreciation of her underlying needs: she is vital, dynamic, sometimes surprisingly insecure, but always aspiring not only to live the good life, but something even more compelling: her own life.

IMPLICATIONS FOR MARKETERS

TRAVEL

Traveling is at the top of the Vibrant Woman's discretionary wish list. But she also travels for work and runs a veritable travel agency, shuttling family members who live in separate locations to and from one another for holidays, visits with the grandchildren, reunions, and more. And she's not just the travel planner; her credit card is likely paying for those trips.

The Vibrant Woman makes her own travel decisions. Even among those who are married, only one-third consult her spouse/partner in choosing travel destinations.[1]

How can marketers appeal to this vibrant traveler?

> **Cater to her desire to learn.** The majority of respondents to a VibrantNation.com survey said they would pay more for trips that include educational components.[2]

> **Keep her busy.** In addition to experiential components, such as meeting locals and "voluntourism," the majority prefer a "moderate" or "extensive" degree of physical activity as part of their travel.

> **Reach her on-line.** While Vibrant Women still consult travel magazines, they do so in smaller numbers, and nearly half of our respondents reported that the Internet is their most important "travel publication."

When it comes to travel, the experience for the Vibrant Woman is about more than sightseeing. Travel is about making friends, connecting with other women, learning about issues and needs in other parts of the world, and using those connections and that knowledge to change the world.

HOME AND GARDEN

Ads showing women 50+ living the carefree life behind gates don't depict anything the Vibrant Woman thinks of as home. If she is contemplating making a move, it's toward a fun urban or residential area that is walking distance to amenities such as restaurants, shopping, and parks or on the fringes of a college campus. These are aspirations that have nothing to do with being taken care of by others and everything to do with turning the page to the next exciting chapter of their lives.[3]

Despite common misperceptions, these Vibrant Women will remain important customers for home furnishing, appliances, and maintenance services. Even if she is simplifying her life, she will be spending significant dollars on improvements, seeking products and services that will make her life easier without compromising style.

She is also an active gardener and expects to remain so forever. Some 83 percent currently garden and expect gardening to remain important to them. While 45 percent are interested in exploring more low-maintenance options, 41 percent say gardening will always be part of their lives. Vibrant Women are willing to put significant dollars toward their gardening. In fact, 89 percent of Boomer women spend up to $500 a year on plants and garden supplies (excluding maintenance).

Fewer than 10 percent of **Vibrant Women** fit the stereotype of a woman planning a move for **health-related reasons** or ceasing to garden because she is "over **it**." In fact, if she is considering any alternative to home ownership herself, it's more likely to be communal living arrangements with like-minded peers–a trend Vibrant Women will fuel over the next decade. Marketers in housing and garden industries should shed the messages that spoke to the Vibrant Woman's parents and offer her solutions that let her remain in control of the spaces that define her.

WINE

Vibrant Women are a key consumer of premium wines. Close to half of VibrantNation.com members report that they generally buy premium wines—those priced at more than $15 a bottle at retail.[5] Because the Vibrant Woman also buys more wine (for herself, for friends and family, for business), she is a far more important and profitable target than winemakers acknowledge in either their marketing plans or advertising.

Because she shops locally (only 18 percent buy wine from megastores, and only 6 percent on-line), smart marketers will be well-served to meet her where she makes her regular rounds. Some 76 percent of our members reported that they buy wine at a neighborhood wine/liquor store or a supermarket (influenced, of course, by whether her state allows supermarkets to sell wine). Because so little beverage industry marketing is directed at them, Vibrant Women rely on their own experience and recommendations from friends when making brand decisions. When asked how they select wines, 75 percent report that they "buy the wines they already like" or make the decision "based on recommendations from friends." This represents a level of brand loyalty well worth further investment. While there is an opportunity to reach Vibrant Women through engaged and friendly retailers (21 percent said they relied on advice from retailers), the fastest route to their hearts and wallets is the advice of friends. Talking to the women themselves about wine—and getting them to talk to each other—is the best way to get them to buy fine wine.

ISSUES AND POLITICS

Vibrant Women vote. And as with consumer purchases, she is also in a position to influence her husband, parents, children, friends, and business associates. Connecting with women over 50 about issues important to them means understanding how they see themselves. When a Vibrant Woman looks in the mirror, she sees someone who is independent, experienced, and engaged. She knows how to make decisions, and she understands there are no perfect answers in life. She is resourceful and savvy when it comes to weighing and balancing pros and cons to find the best possible solution, even to life's most challenging problems. Most important to keep in mind: she doesn't like to be misled and is hard to fool. So here are the simplest tools to utilize with her:

> **Don't scare her.** Sure, she has lots of fear and uncertainty around many political issues, such as entitlement reform and health care. But life has taught her that she will be able to work with or around the issues to make the most out of whatever comes her way. Whatever your position, show her how it will address her concerns. Do not pour oil on the flames of fear, hoping to move her toward your position by using scare tactics or demonizing the opposition's stance.

> **Don't talk down to her.** She is part of the best educated generation of women in history, and what she didn't gain through education she has gained through experience. Insult her intelligence, and you will lose her.

> **Present facts.** She is confident of her ability to make decisions if provided with complete information.

> **Show her you care, and be transparent.** She has great judgment. She can usually tell if people are faking interest in her or not. She doesn't mind if you have a vested interest in the debate; just don't try to hide it.

MEDIA AND ENTERTAINMENT

Vibrant Women are not just the largest and fastest-growing demographic; their patterns of media consumption also make them the most profitable media consumers—and deserving of much more attention.

MUSIC

In addition to topping the music charts, Susan Boyle's success illustrates two important trends: older consumers (and older singers) can drive mass-media events and can do so more profitably than younger consumers. The Boomer women driving Boyle's sales purchased the album almost exclusively in the CD format: only 6 percent purchased it via download.

In a recent VibrantNation.com survey of our members, 94 percent define themselves as music fans, with 40 percent purchasing more than six CDs each year.[5] Given that lost margins on CD sales have driven the music industry into crisis, the industry should be producing more music that appeals to women 50+ and marketing the music it does produce more directly to the women themselves.

MOVIES

Boomer women are also avid (and profitable) movie fans, and Hollywood is starting to notice. *It's Complicated* beat expectations

213

by selling over $22 million in tickets on its Christmas Day release alone. Approximately 72 percent of its audience was female.

Like consumers of all ages, Boomer women reward media companies that give them authentic attention. As a *New York Times* article about Nancy Meyers commented, "In a movie culture consumed by youth and its trappings—vampires, werewolves, stoners, and superheroes—Meyers's decision to pay attention to a part of the population that is often construed (and often construes itself) to be invisible stands out in bold relief. The fact that this decision has proved to be commercially shrewd says something about her instincts as a moviemaker but also says something about a previously unsatisfied hunger, composed of two parts daydream and one part hope, that is finally being addressed."[6]

ELECTRONICS

While media companies scramble to meet the rapidly changing consumption patterns of young consumers, they could both profit and learn from Vibrant Women, who are sustaining the "old school" formats like CDs and cable even while they rapidly adopt newer formats like MP3 players and smartphones. A recent VibrantNation.com survey revealed that almost half listen to downloaded music and one out of four who owns a smartphone uses it to watch videos or movies.[7]

As multi-format consumers, Boomer women could hold the key to sustainability for media companies struggling with the digital age. Delivering more content that appeals to Boomer consumers would reliably increase profits (because Boomers generally rely on higher-margin formats), thereby buying time for media companies to develop profitable business models for younger consumers—and to prepare for the Boomers to go fully digital down the road.

SOCIAL NETWORKING

In chapter 2 we detailed the Vibrant Woman's high level of connectivity, but we can't summarize her "good life" without underlining the role social networking is coming to play in it. Vibrant Women are finding their place on the Web. They are primary users of e-mail, but they are also learning to text. They make their purchases on-line and have signed on to one or another social networking sites.

But this is the moment at which they're also asking: "Now that I'm linked in, what do I do with it?" Those sites that raise the value and lower the barrier will do for women 50+ what the mom-to-mom sites do for younger women. Richard Adler in the new Institute of the Future's landmark study on Boomers agrees that the Web is one of the leading "ecologies of resources"[8] that Boomers will increasingly rely upon to help them share information and pool resources. As members at VibrantNation.com report, it's also a whole lot of fun.

TRADITIONAL MEDIA

In 1976, Barbara Walters (then aged 47) was elevated from the *Today Show* to a role as co-anchor of the *ABC Evening News*. Back then, that was big news.

It's a little surprising that twenty-three years later, when Diane Sawyer (then 63) was named as sole anchor of the *ABC Evening News*, it was still big news. We'd like to think that the elevation of Sawyer, Katie Couric (now 53), and others means that television executives actually recognize that their audience accepts women in the role of network news anchor, a traditional position of authority in American culture. As well they should, given that Boomer women are in large part responsible for keeping traditional media alive, to the degree that newspapers, magazines, and the networks continue to rely on these demographics for sales.

Mainstream media companies, including daily newspapers and television networks, have spent many years wringing their hands over their failure to capture the same market share among 20-somethings that they have long held with Boomers. More recently, these companies have shifted that thinking and realized that the Boomer wave can sustain them for many more years—and at least until another generation of executives has inherited the problem.

What Sawyer's promotion says about culture and news media is interesting, but what it may mean for advertisers is equally noteworthy. Pharmaceutical companies have long used the evening news to reach aging Americans. Other industries should follow, not just because evening news watchers skew older and not just because the networks are betting on older viewers (which they are). Advertisers should connect with female-friendly news programming because the presence of a Vibrant Woman in the anchor chair makes the evening news more of a conversation between women, and nothing motivates Boomer women to try or buy new things more than conversations with each other.

Print and media companies should be sure to keep some of these faces—and voices—employed to speak to their most loyal readers and viewers.

READING

Approximately 40 percent of Boomers have taken up a new hobby or activity in the last few years.[9] Some are traditional—they knit, bake, and garden. Others defy the stereotypes: they take up horseback riding, train for marathons, and learn to fly airplanes.

Some, like their male Boomer counterparts, have even dusted off the old guitar and joined garage rock bands.

But the most commonly shared avocation among Vibrant Women is love of literature. Vibrant Women are big readers. They purchase books at retail, on-line, and through iPads and Kindles to savor when they occasionally have quiet time alone. But reading is also a social experience for them, joining book clubs both in their own communities and on-line. Their tastes are as eclectic as their interests.

While cochairing a panel on "Marketing to Boomer Women" at the 2009 Book Expo America (BEA), we asked the audience by a

---

Some, like their male Boomer counterparts, have even dusted off the old guitar and joined garage rock bands.

---

show of hands, how many of them depend on women 40 up as their primary customer? It was unanimous. We then asked: How many of them would be in jeopardy if this demographic stopped buying books? Again, all hands shot up. Which begs a third question: Why aren't there more books written specifically with Vibrant Women in mind? And even more importantly, why don't more of these books succeed?

Taking into consideration all the obvious explanations, most of which center around ageism and stereotypes among book editors young and old in an industry itself full of Vibrant Women, we see some people in the industry trying hard to get it right. One challenge for the book industry is that by the time they figure out what the Boomer woman wants to read now, this fast-moving demographic is off to the next subject—or at least onto a new and usually unpredictable nuance on the old favorites.

Take Springboard's hit: *How Not to Look Old* by Charla Krupp.[10] Just one year prior, Vibrant Women were embracing the "real woman" movement, and Gail Sheehy was proclaiming "women don't want 60 to be the new 40—they want 60 to be the new 60."[11] About this book's 2009 success, Karen Murgolo of Spring Press explained that *How Not to Look Old* is not promoting looking young—just not looking old. This is an important distinction—and one of the nuances that makes the difference between a best-seller and a bomb.

Why is this generation so hard to read? Because, quite simply, they are defying all expectations of aging, addressing the issues as they arise with fresh perspective and revolutionary zeal. Publishers who think they can figure this demographic out once and for all need to keep listening as Vibrant Women surge onto unmapped territory, making it up as they go along.

AUTOMOBILES

As we noted in our introduction to the book, one way of describing the Vibrant Woman is "post minivan, preretirement." Our research surfaced the information that only 6 percent of our members own a minivan, the utilitarian vehicle associated with the soccer-mom lifestage. Vibrant Women are still mothers, but they are no longer mothers who spend their time shuttling their children between activities. They are buying new cars to symbolize the freedom and discretionary income associated with their new stage of life. She is not shopping to please others, and she is not living off limited resources. Marketers who recognize these facts will likely sell her more sedans or sports cars, offer her more useful professional services, and help her invest her money for a distant and different lifestage ahead.

The jury is still out as to whether automobile companies will wake up to the opportunity Vibrant Women represent while they are still in their prime. Our members let us know, loud and clear, that they feel under-informed, ignored, and often abused by this industry. Individual entrepreneurs, many of them from the Vibrant Woman demographic, have recently been working to bridge that gap. Jody Devere, a dynamic and inspiring Vibrant Woman, has built successful businesses in two male-dominated industries: technology and auto. Her current business, the path-breaking website AskPatty.com, provides deep and detailed information for women car buyers. She also trains and certifies car dealers and services companies in women-friendly practices.

Anne Fleming, another Vibrant Woman, created Women-Drivers.com to provide auto dealers with research on women customers and to allow women to review dealers, the best-rated of which are recognized as "Women-Drivers Friendly." A car-loving dynamo, Fleming notes that women (who generate $200 billion of annual purchasing power for new cars and service) pay an average of $1,250 more for a car than men. Now it's up to the auto industry to erase that disparity or justify the premium paid by its best possible target customer.

SHOPPING AND GIFT EXCHANGE

As we noted in chapter 4, when it comes to Vibrant Women, welcome to the post-shopping era. One of the stereotypes about women as they age is that they take increasing pleasure going shopping in malls and department stores as part entertainment, part personal gratification. Previously, in our chapter on beauty and fashion, we shared our findings that women at 50+ are actually less attracted to shopping as an activity in itself, largely because of poor service from retailers who have let her know in many ways that they prefer younger women as customers.

This doesn't mean she doesn't enjoy the process of researching and scoring just the right item at just the right price. In fact, marketers of luxury brands have coined the term "treasuring" to describe the purchase of high-end goods that will be prized both for their everyday quality and/or for their heirloom potential. More money will be invested in the original purchase of such items, as well as their maintenance and repair. Think Rolex watches, Mephisto shoes, an antique Tiffany lamp, and so on. Whatever joy remains in shopping for her will increasingly center around the

---

Women at 50+ are actually less attracted to shopping, largely because of poor service from retailers.

---

total experience, as in antiquing excursions with girlfriends. In fact, unless shopping can be enhanced by turning it into a special social occasion with others, these days, she is more likely to be doing her shopping on-line.

Changes are also afoot for her, not only in terms of the purchases she makes for herself, but in buying and giving gifts. As she has moved up the motivational pyramid, less concerned about status and trends, she has embraced a spirit of antimaterialism. Over the holidays, when we surveyed our members on the subject of receiving gifts, one-third of them said what they wanted most was "a charitable contribution in their name."[12]

Among other popular answers: almost 20 percent said they wanted the "newest electronic toy or device" (one member named "an iPod and help to use it") and 18 percent said they wanted either "jewelry or clothes." Some 12 percent named books as their preferred gift, and another 24 percent named "other" items like gift cards to stores they like, "cooking stuff," and theatre tickets. The least popular answer: 0 percent (not a single member) said that she wanted "flowers, wine, or fruit."

What the survey tells us is that the Vibrant Woman is more interested in giving back than the market recognizes. And she is less willing to be seen as a passive receptacle for consumables than the market thinks. She may like the contents of a fruit basket, but she apparently doesn't see herself—and doesn't want to be seen—as "the kind of older woman who gets fruit baskets."

The Voices of Vibrant Nation

ON GETTING PAST THE MINIVAN STAGE
FROM A CONVERSATION ON VN

Vibrant Women no longer drive minivans, and they love being able to consider their choices about which car to buy from the perspective of what they want and need.

lovemylife:

I just recently gave up the minivan. I got a crossover. I've had three consecutive minivans and have had enough. My kids are 17 and 19. I was ready for something more "hip." Preretirement? I guess I qualify. We are a huge population and marketers are responding. Hurray!

jhl&f:

We never owned a minivan; we couldn't bring ourselves to take that plunge, I did drive a Suburban for several years, and our daughters laugh about changing into soccer or ballet togs in the "way back" while en route from one appointment or another. I prefer driving a station wagon, a BMW we bought after twenty-five-plus years of marriage. I don't think I will ever shake the need for practicality, but comfort, ease, and, dare I say, luxury have definitely moved up a couple of rungs on the ladder. Our two daughters are now postcollege. I guess I fit loosely into this definition, but I'm still looking for the word about women "of a certain age" being an overlooked and underserved market to leak to not just auto makers but to producers of clothing and personal care products as well. Just because I'm 58 doesn't mean I need to take a laxative drink every night—sheesh!

realestatelady:

Yes, most women under 65 are still working in some form, I would believe, due to the economy, marriage breakdown, or just for future security. The cost of living will not be covered by those without private pensions or ample investment income, so freedom at 55 is not the status quo! Ten years ago I was more ready to retire than I am currently. I have a sweet car, a Vive; it's small but versatile, great on gas, and has a Toyota motor. Cars are the least of my thoughts; to me they are a necessary evil in many ways. I would rather I could ride a horse! Life's journey is the only one we have, and our wheels get us on the road! Let's hope we can afford the damn gas when we're 80!

ON BOOKS AND SOCIABILITY
FROM A CONVERSATION ON VN

"We are all living (at least if you're like me) incredibly full lives, juggling more balls than you can count, and we want community and connection. Joining an on-line book club is a fantastic way to get both."

ONLINE BOOK CLUB STARTING SOON

We who have been posting have agreed to start our own community thru an on-line book club. Our first choice is *Marrying George Clooney* by Amy Ferris.[13] She will join us as she is able... wow! We will start sometime next week. Pick up the book, tell your friends, and let's really talk to one another.

Molly of Matters that Matter:
I am in! We are all living (at least if you're like me) incredibly full lives, juggling more balls than you can count, and we want community and connection. This is a fantastic way to get both. Again, count me in. I am going to share this with every woman I know—and probably some I don't ... think grocery store check-out lines, airplane rides, etc. Can't wait to start the discussion!

Flower Bear:
Ordered my book today and was told it would be in on Monday. It's been a long time since I've done a book club. Can't wait to get started.

Molly of Matters that Matter:
Wonderful! I also loved your profile. The wisdom we accumulate along our own rocky roads is miraculous, and it sounds like you are a wisdom seeker and gatherer and, in doing so, have become wise! Have you read Circle of Stones *yet?[14] It has been around for a long time, and I think you will like it. I'm thrilled that you are going to be joining the* Marrying George Clooney *conversation. It will be a hoot!*

ON PLANNING THE PERFECT TRIP
FROM A CONVERSATION ON VN

Vibrant Women make their own travel plans and love to go on new adventures, especially if there's a learning component to the trip.

Homestaymom:

Cuba This Christmas

We're planning on going to Cuba this Christmas holidays. Does anyone have any tips, suggestions, places to avoid,etc.? I was trying to search cheaptickets.com but Varadero, Cuba, is not a recognized place, any tips?

Jill:

I am a regular to Cuba. I have been there eight times and love it. Your first stop may be to visit www.tripadvisor.com and type in Cub forum. This is a very active website with a lot of helpful information. Cheaptickets.com is an American website, so as a result it doesn't have any trips to Cuba.Try selloffvacations or redtag vacations.

SallyD:

I've been to Cuba, once thru Panama and once from Mexico City. There are loads of great tourist spots, resorts that pick you up at the airport and take you to all-inclusive resorts that'll thrill you, and at a great price.

Try googling "Cuba beach resorts" and forget about America's ridiculous restrictions on Cuba. It's very safe and lovely. I found a bed and breakfast in Havana, for example. Be sure to check out some of Hemingway's favorite haunts, too! And the art market! Oh!

Homestaymom:

Thank you all for your input. I am now getting really excited about this trip. I have been reading all the reviews in Cuba forum and have signed out several books and DVDs from the library. Thank you, Jill and SallyD!

ON TUBING

Boomer women may be conflicted about it, but most spend a fair amount of time watching television.

A friend of mine threw out her TV about two years ago. Just like that. She and her husband said, "Enough"...

I wish I could be like her. I have my "junkie" moments. I really, really like *Dancing with the Stars*, *American Idol*, *Project Runway*, and the Food Network and Home and Garden Television. I was glued to every segment of *America's Got Talent*. *CBS This Morning*, on Sundays, is always full of fascinating feature stories, dealing with arts and culture and goofy tidbits about the human condition. I love that show, too. I guess the common themes are either "underdog becomes top dog" or they teach me something. There is something very helpful and hopeful that just rings my bell.

I don't do soap operas. Or *Dr. Phil*. I've never seen a single episode of *24* or *Desperate Housewives* or *Star Trek*. But I have been known to keep the TV on, on a quiet day, for the "people noises" to keep me company. If there was a waiter in our house, each evening, he would ask, "Will you be having TV with your entree?" The answer would usually be "yes."

The other day, I called my friend to make sure the ban on television was still holding tight—yes, even more so. She made another good point. People often complain that they don't have enough time to get things done, but the average American spends four hours per day/evening in front of the tube, six days each week. Counting on your fingers and toes, that would be twenty-four hours, an entire extra day, each week to find the time to get the things done we can't seem to find the time for. She rested her case. Does anyone have some extra halo polish?

ON LUSTING FOR ELECTRONICS
FROM A CONVERSATION ON VN

When it comes to shopping as entertainment, one of the things Vibrant Women enjoy is electronics. They want to purchase and learn how to operate the latest/hottest products. They also have lots of opinions about how the products are named and marketed.

SeaWriter:

I have such lust for the iPad! I cannot wait until it is available. I thought my MacBook Air was as good as it gets, but this is utterly amazing. I'll still use the MacBook Air for word processing, though, so it's not useless.

Can I tell you how much I regret buying a Kindle just a few weeks ago? I knew immediately it was too cumbersome and unattractive to be something I would use regularly. It's just not beautiful.

pinkim:

I love my Kindle and so do a lot of others!

SeaWriter:

It's a fabulous thing. It holds tons of books, and yes, it's sleek, easy to use, and great for travel. It hardly weighs anything—less than a book by far. It's way cheaper than the iPad, too. I think I paid around $350 for it.

spiritseeker:

And how does everyone feel about the name, "iPad"?

I confess it was the first thing I thought of when I heard the name, too, i.e. feminine hygiene and the mini-pad.

jfalco7:

I'm 56, and the name thing hadn't crossed my mind. I'm not even sure the average twenty-five-year old would know what a "sanitary pad" was. Thank God those days are gone.

jhl&f:

LOL! I had to scroll down to find somebody who had the same thought as I (and my two grown daughters) had. I wondered aloud to a group of women if they came "with a belt." :) Obviously, Steve Jobs needs to make sure there's a girl in the room the next time they start brainstorming what to call the next new gadget.

ON WOMEN 50+ AND WINE
VN INTERVIEW WITH JULIE BROSTERMAN, FOUNDER OF WOMEN & WINE

"One of the things that 50+ women say to me is that coming together with people over sharing a glass of wine, learning about a wine, meeting a winemaker, or doing an experiential event really makes them feel very much alive and in contact with people of all ages."

"Wine means something to women in every stage of their life, whether they're 21 and just coming out of school, or 30 and entertaining business clients for the first time, or Boomers with more time to travel, learn, explore, and connect with like-minded people. One of the things that 50+ women say to me is that coming together with people over sharing a glass of wine, learning about a wine, meeting a winemaker, or doing an experiential event really makes them feel very much alive and in contact with people of all ages. Through Women & Wine, I want to inspire women to make wine an integrated part of their lives in all the ways that you can. I think people would sit around the table longer and have good conversation, which would be amazing for families.

Since starting a company that engages and markets to women, my life and work have become intertwined. I've had incredibly beautiful experiences meeting women who want to share information and collaborate and help one another. As a mortgage banker, I didn't have many women friends. Now I seek out the company of women and rely on them for advice. I'm more emotional in how I communicate. This makes me a better communicator.

My life is more intellectual as well. Sharing a meal with someone over a glass of wine and food, you find that the conversation goes to all aspects of life. Whether it's one-on-one or in groups, it's a much more thoughtful interaction, and that feels really good. I'm very lucky."

[1]"Travel Survey," VibrantNation.com, February 1, 2010, http://www.vibrantnation.com/assets/2510/travel_survey_release_1-25-10.

[2]Ibid.

[3]"Home and Garden Survey,"VibrantNation.com, May 19, 2010, http://www.vibrantnation.com/assets/3020/Vibrant_Nation_home_and_garden_release_final3.pdf. One-third of our respondents reported that they are planning to remain in their current home over the next ten years with a similar number planning to move. The largest percentage (35 percent) is not sure of their plans. Of those who plan to move, 30 percent want to try out a new city/region, another 30 percent want to find a house and/or yard that is easier to maintain, and 17 percent want to be closer to family. Only 8 percent plan to move for health-related reasons.

[4]"Wine Survey," VibrantNation.com, December 8, 2008, http://www.vibrantnation.com/stephen-reily-flash-forward/2009/01/07/underserved-by-premium-brands-reaching-the-wine-buying-woman-50-/.

[5]"Media Consumption Survey," VibrantNation.com, January 6, 2010, http://www.vibrantnation.com/assets/2399/media_consuption_survey_release_1-6-10.pdf.

[6]Daphne Merkkin, "Can Anybody Make a Movie for Women?" *New York Times*, December 15, 2009.

[7]"Tech Survey," Vibrantnation.com, February 25, 2009, http://www.vibrantnation.com/stephen-reily-flash-forward/2009/02/25/vibrantnation-com-tech-survey-boomer-women-are-early-adopters-of-new-consumer-electronics/

[8]Richard Adler, "Boomers: The Next 20 Years—Ecologies of Risk" (report, Institute for the Future in collaboration with MetLife Mature Market Institute, 2006), http://www.metlife.com/assets/cao/mmi/publications/studies/BoomersTheNext20YearsEcologiesofRisk.pdf.

[9]Del Webb, "Age Is Nothing; Attitude Is Everything" (survey, Del Webb, April 13, 2010), http://www.dwboomersurvey.com/.

[10]Charla Krupp, *How Not to Look Old* (New York: Springboard Press, 2008).

[11]Gail Sheehy, "Passage of the Seasoned Woman," (speech, What's Next Boomer Summit, Washington D.C., March 26, 2008).

[12]"Holiday Gift Survey," VibrantNation,com, November 15, 2008, http://www.vibrantnation.com/stephen-reily-flash-forward/2008/11/15/no-more-fruit-baskets-the-vn-gift-survey-and-the-new-anti-materialism/.

[13]Amy Ferris, *Marrying George Clooney: Confessions of a Midlife Crisis*(Berkeley, CA: Seal Press, 2009).

[14]Judith Duerk, *Circle of Stones: Woman's Journey to Herself* (Philadelphia: Innisfree Press, Inc., 1989).

Postscript

THE FUTURE OF MARKETING TO VIBRANT WOMEN

Over the next decade, we will see many millions more women enter the lifestage we have defined here. We know the passion and excitement they will feel about the next long chapter in their lives, and we hope— maybe in some part because of the story they have helped us tell in this book—they will feel a little less of the insecurity that marketers and the media have often imposed on their older sisters.

Throughout this book we've referred to the "Vibrant Woman" alternately as a "Boomer woman" and a "woman 50+." As we conclude, let's pause for a moment to consider what the future is likely to bring in terms of marketing to this promising demographic and whether (and if so, when) the lifestage we have described will ever come to an end.

As we've noted, the term "Boomer" will continue to describe Vibrant Women as long as Boomers dominate the lifestage we've described. By some definitions of Generation X, however, its women will begin turning 50 in 2011, and by any definition, members of Generation X will make up a substantial percentage of Vibrant Women by 2020. Simultaneously, "Boomer" will no longer serve as the synonymous descriptor of this lifestage. Clearly, we believe that Vibrant Nation is new terrain for marketers: a new marketing opportunity that will transcend the influence and dominance of any one generation.

We have said that the condition of being "Vibrant" begins somewhere around age 50. At this moment of history, women seem to share this understanding; almost no woman under 48 has ever joined VibrantNation.com. At the other end, very few women older than 68 join the site, either. Does this mean that being a Vibrant Woman lasts, roughly, from ages 50-70? Does a woman stop being Vibrant at 70?

As you'll expect us to say by now, the answer is complicated.

Today's woman who is already 70+ is in a lifestage that appears to be focused more on the "last thirty years" rather than the Vibrant Woman's dynamic orientation toward the "next thirty years" of her life. A set of concerns and interests built around the changes that occur around 50 may seem pretty distant to a woman whose children themselves may be nearing that age. We expect that is the reason that a woman aged 72 has proven far less likely to join our site than a woman who is still in her 50s or 60s.

But we also believe this is going to change. Although VibrantNation.com is a young site itself, we don't expect to see women drop off our membership rolls just because they are turning 70. As we've made it clear by now, a Vibrant Woman is in a lifestage more than an age range, and a lifestage doesn't suddenly end on a particular birthday.

While some purchasing patterns of the Vibrant Woman may change and even decline somewhat as she ages into her 70s and 80s, in the intervening years the Vibrant Woman will also have come into the largest transfer of generational wealth in human history— by some estimates an inheritance of up to $40 trillion. That alone will transform her ability and need to give back, manage money, acquire and sell real estate, and spend money on her children and grandchildren. Marketers who want to do business with this Vibrant consumer (often left holding investments from all the people likely to predecease her, including her parents, her husband, and his parents) can certainly engage her by following the lessons we and she shared with you in this book.

While many women may indeed become less vibrant as they age, they will continue to redefine what it means to be 70, 80, and 90 just as they redefined what it meant to be 40, 50, and 60. We look forward to hearing them describe that new lifestage —one we think will see them mounting another stage or two up the developmental pyramid we described in chapter 3 as they remind marketers that every year of increased longevity means another year of business opportunities and an extension of this dynamic woman's search for new answers to her needs.

At the same time, we will see many millions more women, both trailing-edge Boomers as well as Generations X and eventually their daughters in Generation Y, enter the lifestage we have defined here. We know the passion and excitement they will feel about the next long chapter in their lives, and we hope—maybe in some part because of the story they have helped us tell in this book—they will feel a little less of the insecurity that marketers and the media have often imposed on their older sisters.

Rewarding the Vibrant Nation will generate unlimited business opportunities, for sure, but it will also help women in this dynamic lifestage achieve their genuine goals of continuing to grow as they age and to keep changing not only our understanding of what it means to be a Vibrant Woman 50+, but also the world's.

Sources/Resources

FROM THE EXPERTS:

Here are some of our favorite books from the last ten years about marketing to Boomers, women, and both.

Barletta, Marti. *PrimeTime Women: How to Win the Hearts, Minds, and Business of Boomer Big Spenders.* Chicago: Kaplan Business, 2007.

Brennan, Bridget. *Why She Buys: The New Strategy for Reaching the World's Most Powerful Consumers.* New York: Crown Business, 2009.

Brown, Mary, and Carol Orsborn, *BOOM: Marketing to the Ultimate Power Consumer—The Baby-Boomer Woman.* New York: AMACOM, 2006.

Dychtwald, Maddy. *Influence: How Women's Soaring Economic Power Will Transform Our World for the Better.* New York: Voice, 2010.

Dychtwald, Ken. *Age Power: How the 21st Century Will Be Ruled by the New Old.* New York: Tarcher, 2000.

Furlong, Mary. *Turning Silver into Gold: How to Profit in the New Boomer Marketplace* Upper Saddle River, NJ: FT Press, 2007.

Green, Brent. *Marketing to Leading-Edge Baby Boomers: Perceptions, Principles, Practices & Predictions.* Ithaca, NY: Paramount Market Publishing, Inc., 2006.

Nyren, Chuck. *Advertising to Baby Boomers.* Ithaca, NY: Paramount Market Publishing, Inc., 2007.

Quinlan, Mary Lou, Jen Drexler, and Tracy Chapman. *What She's Not Telling You: Why Women Hide the Whole Truth and What Marketer's Can Do about It.* New York: Just Ask a Woman Media, 2009.

Silverstein, Michael, Kate Sayre, and John Butman. *Women Want More: How to Capture Your Share of the World's Largest, Fastest-Growing Market.* New York: HarperBusiness, 2009.

Skoloda, Kelley. *Too Busy to Shop: Marketing to Multi-Minding Women.* Westport, CT: Praeger Publishers, 2009.

Thornhill, Matt, and John Martin. *Boomer Consumer: Ten New Rules for Marketing to America's Largest, Wealthiest and Most Influential Group.* Great Falls, VA: LINX Corp., 2007.

Weigelt, David, and Jonathan Boehman. *Dot Boom: Marketing to Baby Boomers through Meaningful Online Engagement.* Great Falls, VA: LINX Corp., 2009.

Wolfe, David B. *Ageless Marketing Strategies for Reaching the Hearts and Minds of the New Customer Majority.* Chicago: Kaplan Business, 2003.

About VibrantNation.com

VibrantNation.com is the leading on-line community devoted exclusively to the influential and fast-growing demographic of smart, successful women 50+. Launched in January 2009, VibrantNation.com has seen rapid growth and now represents the largest website devoted to this demographic. At Vibrant Nation, these women (whom we've named "Vibrant Women") can look for tips, share information, and join in smart conversations about work, style, relationships, wellness, books, and more.

Vibrant Women represent the healthiest, wealthiest, best-educated generation of women in history, yet their real strengths and interests are generally ignored in the marketplace. As a result, Vibrant Women rely even more than others on support and information from other women like them when making important decisions. Like a "mom" site, VibrantNation.com recognizes that when women enter a new lifestage their most important resource is a place to connect with other women like them. VibrantNation.com is the place where they can discuss the issues they are passionate about with women like them.

About the Authors

STEPHEN REILY

Stephen Reily, entrepreneur, marketing expert, and active blogger, founded VibrantNation.com, the leading online community exclusively devoted to the influential and fast-growing Boomer demographic of smart, successful women over 50, after researching the lack of media geared toward women 50+ and spending years listening to women themselves identify their interests and needs.

As a marketing professional, Stephen built IMC Licensing, a brand-licensing agency, and is responsible for overseeing licensing strategy and relationships with IMC's clients, like Kraft Foods and Anheuser Busch, as well as IMC's business development and marketing efforts. Stephen has also published articles in *Brandweek* and brandchannel.com among others and has been a featured speaker at leading industry events, including Aging in America, Book Expo America, the Educational Travel Conference (ETC), the Licensing Letter Symposium, Licensing University, Marketing to Women (M2W), Silvers Summit at CES, and What's Next Boomer Summit.

Stephen graduated from Yale College, summa cum laude, and from Stanford Law School, after which he clerked for Justice John Paul Stevens of the U.S. Supreme Court. He lives in Louisville, Kentucky, with his wife and three children.

CAROL ORSBORN, PH.D.

Dr. Carol Orsborn is an internationally recognized author, blogger, and thought leader on issues related to Boomer women, adult development, and work/life balance. Carol is senior strategist with VibrantNation.com, the leading on-line community exclusively devoted to smart, successful women over 50. A public relations veteran, she cofounded the first initiative by a global PR firm dedicated to helping companies market to the Boomer generation. A pioneer of the business and consciousness movement, Carol has written over fifteen books on the connection between success and quality of life, including *Boom: Marketing to the Ultimate Power Consumer—the Baby Boomer Woman* (coauthored with Mary Brown) and *The Art of Resilience.*

Speaking to and for her generation, Carol has appeared on Oprah and The Today Show, multiple times, and in the pages of *People Magazine* and *The New York Times*, among many others. In addition, she has been a speaker at Aging in America, Book Expo America, the Educational Travel Conference (ETC), the Florida Boomer Lifestyle Conference, PRSA's Counselor's Academy, the National Conference on Positive Aging, Marketing to Women (M2W), and What's Next Boomer Summit.

Carol received her Ph.D. from Vanderbilt University, studying adult development and ritual studies, including intergenerational values formation and transmission. She has taught ethics and values-driven leadership, serving on the faculties of Georgetown University, Vanderbilt University's Leadership Development Center of the Owen Graduate School of Management, Loyola Marymount University, and the Doctoral Program in Organizational Leadership at Pepperdine University's Graduate School of Educational and Psychology. Dr. Orsborn lives in Los Angeles and Brooklyn and is a wife, mother of two adult children, and a new grandmother.

An invitation to contact the authors
   Stephen@vibrantnation.com
   Carol@vibrantnation.com

LaVergne, TN USA
31 October 2010
202717LV00002BC